Kirsten Wolf

Games and
Sports for Dogs

BARRON'S

CONTENTS

3 Dog sports for four-legged athletes

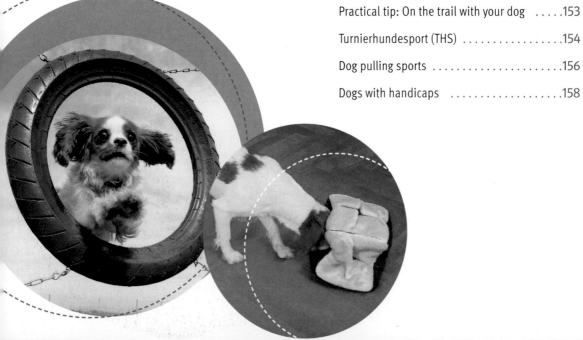

4 Happy and healthy

5 Games and sports at a glance

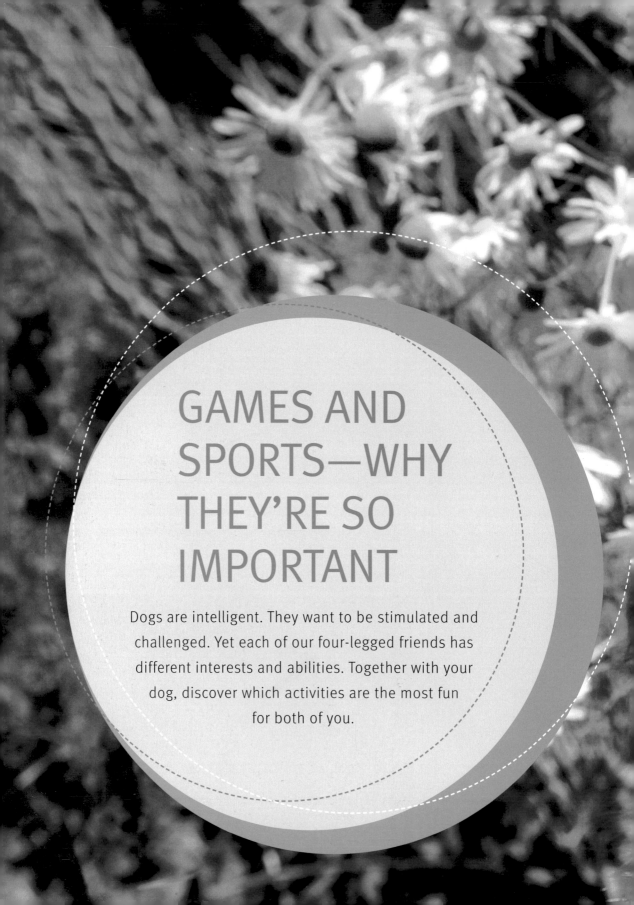

GAMES AND SPORTS—WHY THEY'RE SO IMPORTANT

Dogs are intelligent. They want to be stimulated and challenged. Yet each of our four-legged friends has different interests and abilities. Together with your dog, discover which activities are the most fun for both of you.

It All Depends on the **Right Activity**

We humans are our dogs' best friends. This certainly comes as no surprise to you as a dog owner—after all, you experience it every day. You make your four-legged friend happiest when you have time for him. This fact is unique in behavioral biology: There is really no other species that prefers humans to their own kind as social partners. This certainly doesn't mean that dogs don't need other dogs—quite the contrary. Regular interaction—playing together—is important for a dog's normal

development and his ability to behave appropriately when dealing with other dogs. Yet without his human partner's loving care, the dog's social development will suffer. Our four-legged friends need us. They rely on us for more than just food and health. In particular, their peace of mind, steady temperament, and friendliness depend on whether we, which is to say their people, care about them, spend time with them, and teach them to be our companions in the world we share with them.

From working partner to playmate

The origin and history of the domestic dog illustrate how his status in human society has changed over the centuries. From a wolf living in a pack, he evolved to become man's trusty helper. He accompanied his master on hunts, flushed game, and retrieved it—always working together closely with his human partner. His ability to communicate made him an asset in many other activities. The dog herded and guarded livestock, he protected house and farm, he pulled sleds and milk carts—and he became an indispensable pal, someone who could share not only the day's toil, but also its joys and sorrows. He is still our friend, but society has changed. Following the transformation of society from agrarian to industrial, the dog now finds himself out of work in the Information Age.

He has joined the ranks of the unemployed. At least this is true for modern societies that have already made the transition and have conferred a

Little dog, big treat: Many dogs love playing ball more than anything else. That's why it's an ideal reward after a task that demands concentration.

Have fun learning: This young dog tests his courage against a homemade pole with fluttering banners.

different status on their pets today. The modern dog is no longer a working partner; instead, he is primarily a social and recreational companion. He shares our home with us like a member of the family.

What dogs and people enjoy

For true dog lovers, our four-legged friend's "unemployment" is a serious challenge, because in our hectic lives we sometimes underestimate our pet's need for activity. It's really not so difficult to dispel animal boredom, though. The dog's intelligence and close relationship with humans make it possible to include him actively in many areas of life, whether it's going for a walk or staying home, on the weekend, on vacation, or even in the office.

There are countless activities that are sure to be lots of fun not just for your dog, but for you, too. We'll introduce you to a whole series of them in this book: dog sports like agility, flyball, disc dog events, canine freestyle, or obedience; recreational sports where your dog can accompany you, like bicycling, hiking, swimming, or jogging; and any number of games that you can easily fit into your day—from simple find-the-treat games like the

"Towel Roll" (❯ pages 22/23) to clever tricks like "Jump Through the Hoop" (❯ pages 62/63), and difficult mental exercises like the "Shell Game" (❯ pages 91/93).

❯ pages 22/23 ❯ pages 62/63 ❯ pages 91/93

 PRACTICAL TIP

Bad moods are taboo

Dogs can read our moods. If we're irritated because a step in a game didn't work out the way we wanted, this affects them like a cold shower—after all, they trusted us and let us motivate them. When you're playing a game, though, the most important thing should be having fun together, not seeing that everything goes without a hitch. Scale back your demands to the point that your dog can follow you again, and never forget to praise him sincerely when he succeeds in doing something.

Every dog is unique

If you have a dog of a specific breed, you usually know what traits your four-legged friend has inherited; i.e., what's in his genes. Owners of mixed-breed dogs try to find out which breeds were probably involved in the mix in order to infer something about their dog's possible tendencies and preferences. This is a good way to get a better idea of your own dog, so you can offer him appropriate activities. And yet every dog, whether purebred or mixed breed, is unique. Your four-legged friend's individual personality plays an important role in determining what he likes and what he's not so fond of, what he can succeed at right away and what takes him a little bit longer. Another factor is his puppyhood: His experiences as a puppy and young dog, what he learned or didn't learn in the first weeks and months of his life, may have a greater influence on his behavior than anything else. That's why all dog owners, whether they got their dog as a puppy or didn't become his "parents" until later, need to observe their four-legged friend carefully.

The right activity for every canine individualist

Try to understand your dog's reactions. Notice how he expresses frustration and joy, what seems to be beyond him, and what he finds especially easy or difficult. Then you can choose just the right thing for him, whether game or sport, from among the wide range of activities available. Although it's good to be sensitive to your dog's needs, don't forget to consider your own interests when making a choice. Only when a game or sport is truly enjoyable for both of you—dog and owner—will it be perfect. Take time to experiment: If agility is not a good fit, then maybe you'd both have more fun with tracking—or you might take a canine freestyle class and discover it's just the thing for your "four-legged star."

Many dog schools and clubs offer such an assortment of games and sports today that you're certain to find what you're looking for and, with professional instruction, become a first-rate coach for your four-legged friend. In order to make it easier for you to choose among the games and decide just what suits your time and training schedule, we have divided them into five different categories.

Food games—simple and tasty

Food games appeal to most dogs because a tasty treat is always welcome now and then.

In these games, our four-legged friends can earn a part of their daily food ration if they are attentive and clever; at the same time, they learn that it really pays to concentrate when they're with you. Besides, these games are usually so simple and employ such everyday household objects that they can easily be squeezed into your schedule on occasion to provide a little variety in the daily routine for both of you. In addition, they are even suitable for puppies and don't demand too much of four-legged senior citizens, either (❯ from page 18).

Searching and fetching games for super sleuths

These games can quickly become addictive: Many dogs love the opportunity to put their superb olfactory abilities to the test and really astound their master in the process. It's a fantastic experience to watch your own dog suddenly picking up a scent (laid down just for him) or following the scent trail of a stranger. Some of these games require a little more time and patience for the dog to understand and be able to carry out every step. Naturally, this manual offers you searching and fetching games that will provide a bit of fun indoors or outdoors: A little "Treasure Hunt," for example, or "Find the Scented Towel" (❯ from page 31).

Take a break! Every walk with your dog will become more exciting for both of you if you include a few pleasant breaks for active games.

PRACTICAL TIP

Set up a vocabulary notebook

"Stay!" "Stop!" "Halt!" —What?! It's important to give your four-legged friend clear signals. This is true for both the verbal commands and the gestures that you use to communicate with him. It's a good idea to set up a little vocabulary notebook where you enter every signal (and how to do each one) that your dog has learned from you or other family members. The advantage of a book like this is that anyone can look up all the commands the dog has mastered as well as how to give them correctly. You'll be amazed at how many words you collect!

Active games to stay in shape

These games don't just keep your dog fit; they also make walks more interesting.

In addition, they fulfill a basic need of our dogs, which, after all, were originally cursorial animals, adapted for running. It's not just a matter of speed or stamina, but also the ability to pay close attention to the requirements of the game and to carry them out precisely. If you're always coming up with little games when you're out with your dog, you'll stay exciting for him and have an easier time getting even a somewhat distractible dog to focus his attention on you (❯ from page 52).

Tricks for four-legged stars

Learning little tricks with your four-legged friend is a good opportunity to demonstrate just how well the two of you work as a team. Without pressure or drills, the two of you are practicing amazing moves that only work if both you and your dog are completely focused on the task at hand. Many of the

tricks—once they have been thoroughly rehearsed—can become part of your everyday routine and thus provide a welcome change of pace, whether at home, during a walk, or as part of a training session in the backyard or park (❯ from page 68).

Thinking games to stay mentally fit

These games are especially good for getting our four-legged friend's little gray cells working. What's important here is reasoning. Dogs are extremely intelligent, as shown by their ability to remember, and they can recognize cause and effect. Find out for yourself how quickly your dog comprehends.

Don't forget, though, that thinking is hard work; this is as true for animals as it is for people. That's why you should always use moderation when putting even these supposedly quiet games on the play schedule and then provide for relaxation afterward—for example, with a walk or a few minutes of romping around (❯ page 47).

Pay attention to each other

The wonderful thing about all these activities is that playing together also means learning together. The more you interact with your dog, the better you'll be able to interpret his reactions correctly and guide him using clear signals and unambiguous body language (❯ Practical tip, page 11). In the process, your dog is training his ability to concentrate and his stamina as well as his discipline.

He will become an attentive companion who can't wait to see what you'll think up next for him.

Playing without stress

Keeping your dog entertained from dawn to dusk is not the idea here. Dogs need to rest, just as we do, and like us, they have a right to it. When you decide to spend your time engaged in activities with your dog, it should not lead to stress. On the contrary, what's important is that you enjoy being together, recognize what your dog actually needs, and guide and train his abilities in such a way that he is happy—and also that he leaves you in peace when you don't have time for him. You'll find a little trick on how to make this clear even to play "fanatics" in the Practical Tip on page 19. Make sure to adjust your program of games and sports to the temperament, age, and personality of your dog and, naturally, to the rhythm of your own life as well. Your life doesn't have to revolve around your dog.

Bull's eye: With a little imagination, you can come up with many simple ideas for games that your dog will enjoy—like this precise *down* inside a hula hoop.

Happy to be alive: Dogs are happy if they can satisfy their need for activity with games and sports.

Instead, he needs a balanced mixture of various stimulating activities and rest periods. This includes adequate social contact with other dogs, walks with plenty of opportunity to let off steam and nose around, encounters with other people, and a well-chosen program of activities that suit your dog's temperament as well as your own.

For this reason it is also very important not to overdo your demands in games and sports. Introduce the games gradually and without rushing; it's better to postpone a new step in an exercise for another day. When playing with your dog, always remember to end on a positive note. If something works really well, celebrate enthusiastically with your dog and be content with this little triumph—that's always a more effective method of reinforcing what your dog has learned than ambition, which overtaxes your four-legged friend's motivation and ability to learn. Your goal shouldn't be speedy success, but rather having fun, enjoying each other's company, and forging a strong mutual bond; this will make your dog confident, easy to get along with, and happy—in short, the dog of your dreams.

 PRACTICAL TIP

Never play alone!

If you watch your dog playing "Spin the Bottle," for example (❯ pages 24/25), you'll see why you should always be there to supervise when he's busy with a game: Depending on where he's playing, the dog may quickly maneuver the bottle into a corner or under a dresser and won't be able to get it out again by himself. Even the activity where you hide treats in a box (❯ page 19) can—if things go wrong—become a trap. Regardless of which activity you are doing with your dog, never leave him alone with his task; instead, always keep him company. This way you can intervene immediately if he happens to get into frustrating or even dangerous situations.

Meant for each other: The most beautiful gift that you can receive in return for your time and attention is a deep and trusting bond with your dog.

 PRACTICAL TIP

Pure relaxation: romping and cuddling

Concentrating is hard work for humans and animals alike. That's when free play like a simple tug-of-war, a little roughhousing on the ground, or throwing a ball or a toy is the perfect way for both of you to relax. Take a break for this sort of play, especially if you feel that a game or athletic activity has demanded a lot of brainwork from your dog. Of course, you always have to make sure that the dog doesn't overstep his bounds: Don't let him get overexcited and hide the ball or toy from you like prey instead of giving it back to you. And if your dog likes to cuddle, be happy about it and treat him frequently to a few minutes of affectionate petting or a little massage (❯ page 169).

Test: Does Your Dog Trust You?

The following questions should help you gauge your relationship with your dog on the "bond barometer."

1. **When I take my dog for a walk without a leash . . .**

   A ⬤ . . . he always stays near me
   B ⬤ . . . he sometimes disappears from view
   C ⬤ . . . he goes his own way, sometimes far away from me

2. **When I speak to my dog by name . . .**

   A ⬤ . . . he always looks at me expectantly
   B ⬤ . . . I can tell by his posture that he has heard me, but I often have to speak to him a second or third time to get him to look at me
   C ⬤ . . . he frequently does not respond at all

3. **I can touch my dog anywhere on his body without having him react defensively (growling, snarling, snapping)**

   A ⬤ always true
   B ⬤ almost always true
   C ⬤ rarely true

4. **My dog performs the exercises that he has mastered . . .**

   A ⬤ . . . willingly at all times
   B ⬤ . . . often somewhat reluctant (has to be asked)
   C ⬤ . . . reluctantly, as if he doesn't enjoy it

5. **When my dog is frightened or worried by something . . .**

   A ⬤ . . . he immediately looks at me, as if to say: "What do you think about that?"
   B ⬤ . . . he doesn't necessarily come to me
   C ⬤ . . . he sometimes runs away from it

INTERPRETATION

Which answers occur most frequently: A, B, or C?

(A) Clearly defined roles: Your dog feels safe with you and knows you understand him, so he's happy to cooperate with you. He accepts you as the team leader and always tries hard to please you. Don't take this for granted: Never forget to praise him for his motivated participation.

(B) The "Yes, but . . . " type: Sometimes things goes smoothly, but other times he seems to have forgotten everything: Your dog usually focuses on you, but once in a while he prefers to make up his own mind—perhaps because your instructions aren't clear. You have to set the tone calmly and kindly but firmly. That works especially well in games and sports, because consistency and fun go hand in hand here.

(C) Show me the way . . .: Perhaps your dog is still young, or you haven't had him very long. However, it may be that he is just a particularly independent sort (which can certainly be a breed characteristic). All that may explain why he has not yet found his place in the team. With the right motivation and the experience of achieving success together in games or sports, you will gradually strengthen your relationship with your four-legged friend. And that is exactly what he wants: A close, loving bond with you that gives him sufficient freedom, but also security and direction.

15

GAMES FOR INDOORS AND OUTDOORS

It's time to play! Your four-legged friend senses that, right now, you are all his. He is overjoyed because there's nothing better than playing with you, basking in your praise, and—as an added bonus—earning a few tasty treats.

Food Games— Simple and Tasty

Most dogs develop a real taste for these games. What's required here are a good sense of smell, agility, and intelligence; and don't forget patience, because the search doesn't begin until you give the signal to start! The games are simple: You need food treats and items like towels, cardboard boxes, or plastic bottles—in other words, ordinary household objects. That's why food games are ideal for providing a few minutes of fun occasionally. You don't need a lot of preparation time, and, in any case, two or three rounds are plenty. Our treat games take place indoors—and for good reason: The next time you take your dog for a walk, you certainly don't want him picking up everything

that looks edible and thus creating his own food game. When you're outdoors, make it a rule to reward him from a treat bag, or use it when you have him search for food (❯ page 38). This way, you can be consistent about teaching your dog not to start his own treat hunt when you're out with him.

In case it's hard to whet your dog's ambition with the usual treats, resort to food rewards that you hand out fairly seldom, like a piece of dried liver or cooked bits of chicken, some microwaved love-sodium hot dog, or a bit of cheese. And in case your four-legged friend turns his nose up at treats, simply hide his favorite toy.

Cardboard Box and Pillow Pile

 What this trains: All dogs like a tasty treat now and then. Here they have to work for it using agility and a bit of persistence. It's worth the effort!

What you need: Some food treats, a medium-sized cardboard box, newspaper, and two or three pillows.

Take an empty cardboard box that's the right size for your dog. Your four-legged friend should be able to rummage around in it easily with her nose. Remove staples, bits of plastic, and similar hazards. Crumple up a few sheets of newspaper and put them in the box. Add a few food treats. Let the dog watch as you do this. Some dogs may find the box scary at first, so don't bury the treats too deep. Later, you can increase the degree of difficulty by hiding just one treat (but make it a bigger one), adding more newspaper, and burying the treat(s) deeper.

First *sit*, then search

Get your dog in the *sit* or *down* position and place the box an arm's length away from her on the floor. If you have a puppy who has not yet mastered this basic exercise, start by distracting her a bit at first so that she doesn't make a dash for the box on her own. Then give your dog the command, for example *"Find it!"* Now the dog can root around in the box to her heart's content and nab one treat after another. Depending on her temperament, she may go about it with quiet concentration or wild

PRACTICAL TIP

You decide when it's time to play

To let your dog know when it's time to play and when playtime is over, decide on a start and a stop signal that you will use consistently. It could be *"Let's play!"* to start and *"All done!"* or *"That's all!"* to finish. After you give the signal to stop, never let yourself be coaxed into playing one more round just because your dog looks so cute. You are the boss here, and you have to keep it that way.

enthusiasm. It's fun to see which technique the dog uses: Does she go about the search deliberately, nosing among the balls of newspaper, or does she simply knock over the box? Does she dig through the papers with her paws? Does she even jump into the box in order to get as close to the tasty quarry as possible? Anything that helps her find the treats is permissible. However, you should intervene if the dog gets too boisterous and starts to rip up the newspaper. That's not the point of the game. In this case, call off the treat hunt; later on, you can try again to teach your four-legged friend the rules of the game (❯ Expert tip, page 31).

Something tasty in the pillow pile

Start small: In the beginning, place a treat on the pillow and, when you give your dog the signal, let her pick it up. She'll quickly grasp what this game is all about. Then, gradually increase the size of the pillow pile.

Now, depending on how clever and courageous the dog is, you can hide the treats between two, three, or even four pillows. Here, too, if something frightens her, make it simpler. If knocking over three pillows startles her, then start with just two pillows so that she gradually gets used to the instability of the pile. Naturally, biting the pillows is against the rules; otherwise, the game must be called off. Give your dog time to search, and praise her as she goes about it. Let her take her time trying to find the best way to tackle the pile. Two or three rounds of this game are plenty. Give a stop signal to end the game (❯ Practical tip, page 19).

Tip: After the game, put away the cardboard box and the pillows so that the dog is not tempted to try a little game without you. After all, what's important here is doing the activity together. And don't forget: Subtract the treats from your dog's daily food ration.

1. The temptation: Amy sits in front of the box, still a bit mistrustful, but she finds the contents very enticing. The dog just watched her owner hiding treats in the box!

2. Approach cautiously: Now go for the box! After she gets the start signal *"Find it!,"* the three-year-old Irish Terrier begins by investigating the situation cautiously.

3. Nothing to fear: Her courage has paid off. Hidden among all the newspaper, she discovers her favorite little dried treats. Not so bad, this game.

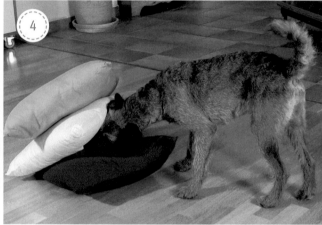

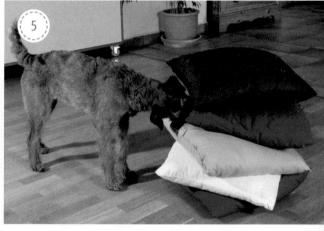

4. Something tasty in the pillow pile: Amy pokes her nose straight into the soft pile of pillows, where there's a surprise in store on every level.

5. Change the height of the pile: When the dog is no longer startled by knocking over the pillows, you can go higher. To make the game more challenging for a super sleuth, don't hide treats between all the pillows.

21

Towel Roll

 What this trains: Sense of smell, patience, and—naturally—agility, because before the dog can enjoy the treats, she must first develop the correct technique.

What you need: A few treats and an old hand towel.

A hand towel can be very exciting—at least when it smells like tasty treats! But how do you get to the good stuff? Your four-legged friend will quickly realize that a very special technique is required here.

First, though, the dog has to wait until the towel roll is released for the treasure hunt. Then the dog sniffs eagerly at the roll and makes a startling discovery: There's something inside!

Start out simply

To make sure that your dog succeeds as soon as possible, don't hide the treat deep inside the roll at first; instead, place it closer to the end of the towel.

Now the dog sets to work with nose or paws and tries to discover which technique will yield the desired result. Let her take her time experimenting in the beginning. Meanwhile, praise her enthusiastically for showing so much patience and persistence. Later, you can increase the degree of difficulty by hiding the treat deeper and deeper inside the roll until finally the entire towel must be unfurled before the dog gets to the coveted treat.

Roll, don't shake

If your little smarty-pants simply shakes the towel or pushes it around with her nose so that the treat falls out, call off the game. The next time, place the desired morsel so close to the end of the roll that even a little nudge with her nose unrolls the towel enough to reveal the treat. If that doesn't work, give your four-legged friend some help.

Unroll the towel a bit right before her eyes until the dog understands the roll technique and tries it herself. When she finds the treat, praise her enthusiastically for her discovery, and pick up the towel so that she doesn't play with it.

By the way, this game is especially good for older dogs, too, because they quickly find the treat with just a few gentle movements and don't have to overexert themselves in the process.

1. Hide the treat: This towel is reserved for playtime with Amy. In the beginning, the treat is hidden fairly close to the end of the roll so that the dog finds it quickly.

2. Successful search: Because she only has to unroll the towel a little bit with her nose in order to find the treat, it never occurs to Amy to shake the towel. That wasn't so hard.

3. Refine the technique: Keep on going. The dog understands what she has to do in order to reach the treat. She unrolls the hand towel a bit more by herself.

4. Increase the degree of difficulty: Amy doesn't lose patience, even when the roll is slow to give up the treat. The dog doesn't quit until her nose work finally pays off.

Treat Bottle

 What this trains: Sense of smell, agility, and persistence.

What you need: A sturdy plastic bottle and a handful of kibble or small, dry treats that will fit through the opening of the bottle.

In this game, your four-legged friend has to earn his food.

"Spin the bottle"

Take some of your dog's daily ration of dry food (or all of it, depending on how much food is required) and pour it into a sturdy, medium-sized plastic bottle. The opening shouldn't be so big that the food falls out at the slightest spin. Make sure the neck of the bottle doesn't have sharp edges that could hurt the dog. Start by having the dog wait patiently in the *sit* or *down* position. Now place the open, filled bottle in the middle of the room and let the dog begin the game. The dog will approach the bottle inquisitively and make an initial attempt to get at the treats. If he is too timid about it, show him how it works by moving the bottle a little until something falls out. Now, he'll probably show an amazing amount of energy and inventiveness in order to get to the treats himself. Perhaps he will pick up the bottle in his mouth and discover that—when the opening is on the bottom—something falls out. Or he will shove it around vigorously with his paw or nose. He may try to bite the bottle, which is why it should be very sturdy. How much effort the dog has to expend depends on the size of the kibble. You can also have the game require more agility and patience by putting slightly larger morsels in the bottle for the next round.

Variations from the pet store

One toy available at the pet store—a sturdy bottle with a rope inside—presents a very special challenge for the dog (❯ photo, left). Or you may decide on a treat ball made of bite-resistant material with adjustable openings, which increases he degree of difficulty. For a quiet version, there are fabric cubes that can be filled with treats. However, the openings on the sides of the cubes are so large that it's better to put a treat stick or a larger biscuit inside.

1. A challenge: You can buy this treat bottle in the pet store. The dog has to remove in the rope before he can get to the treats inside.

2 Quiet version: Fabric cubes that can be filled with treats, like this one, make very little noise when the dog plays with them. If you can take your dog to work, this is a wonderful way to keep him busy.

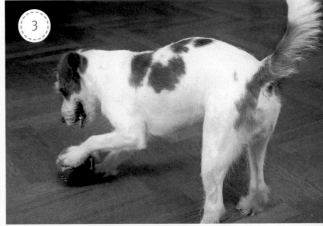

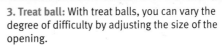

3. Treat ball: With treat balls, you can vary the degree of difficulty by adjusting the size of the opening.

4. Homemade version: An empty plastic bottle can easily be filled with dry treats. At first, use just small pieces that roll out easily so that the dog succeeds quickly.

Treat Flip

 What this trains: Discipline and agility are required here because the dog must wait patiently until she gets the signal to *flip*—then she is allowed to catch the treat deftly in midair.

What you need: Pieces of dry food or cheese cubes that are not too light.

Some dogs love to practice this little trick in order to get a coveted treat, and they really give it their all; for others, it's just too much trouble. See how your four-legged friend reacts to the Treat Flip.

Every moment is rewarded

A prerequisite for this game is that the dog can remain in the *sit* position, because she must start by holding very still with the treat on her nose. In the first step, you teach your dog to leave the treat on her nose. To do that, gently grasp her muzzle and place the treat far forward on her nose. If she holds this position for even just a moment, take the treat

from her nose and give it to her as a reward for her patience.

Now, you have to increase her staying power by few seconds. Try it two or three times in succession and repeat this exercise for a few days until you're certain the dog can wait patiently with the reward on her nose.

A short signal for the *flip*

Now for the next step. Decide on a short signal or sound, for example *"Flip!"* or *"Catch!"* Even snapping your fingers loudly serves the purpose. Place the treat on the dog's nose as described above and take two steps back. Facing your dog, say the command or snap your fingers and raise your arms in an inviting gesture. With a little luck, the dog will throw back her head and try to catch the treat. If it doesn't work at first, pick up the treat and try again.

Her first success: Great!

Repeat the attempt only two or three times, no more, and don't forget to praise your four-legged friend enthusiastically—even if the Treat Flip is still not right. Of course, she still gets the treat at the end because she has certainly earned a reward for her participation. Over the next few days, keep trying the exercise.

As soon as the dog does it correctly, shower her with praise. As you'll see, that's almost more effective for motivating your pet than giving her the treat. You can also help her master the knack of catching a treat in midair by simply tossing treats to her a few times.

1. Place the treat: Amy the Beauceron and her owner make a great team. The dog readily allows a treat to be placed on her nose.

2. Wait patiently: Every time she holds still, Amy gets the treat from her nose as a reward. Finally, the exercise works perfectly: Amy waits patiently with the treat on her nose until the signal comes.

Don't use force!

Of course, if your dog shows that she doesn't like this game at all, for example, if she turns her head aside or walks away, then it's better if you pick a different food game; for example, "Cardboard Box and Pillow Pile" on page 19 or "Towel Roll" on page 22. Don't force your four-legged friend to practice something that she obviously finds unpleasant. When you and your dog play games together, having fun should always take priority.

3. Successful flip: It didn't work at first, but Amy and her owner practiced diligently. After a few tries, the treat flies into the air and the dog catches it deftly.

Children and Dogs

Children love to play, and so do most dogs. Nevertheless, there are definite rules for playing together that will protect everyone involved and ensure that nothing spoils their fun.

Dogs make children strong, as studies have confirmed. A pet can foster self-confidence in a child if the two share a strong bond and can even protect the child from depression, because a four-legged buddy provides a feeling of closeness and warmth. First, though, the relationship between child and dog must be characterized by fairness and respect. Neither one should demand too much of the other. For parents, this means staying nearby and keeping your eyes and ears open, because the children don't have "top dog" status for their four-legged friends. They lack the assertiveness and clear body language for it. Besides, when they play together, a dog is often physically superior to a child. And if things get out of hand, children sometimes start to shriek or simply run away, which can lead to unfortunate misunderstandings with the dog.

It's good to be close, but always make sure that the dog doesn't feel harassed. The child can hug the dog, but squeezing is not allowed. As a rule, children are not yet able to interpret the dog's appeasement signals correctly. Unfortunately, this often leads to dangerous misunderstandings between dog and child.

My teddy bear, your teddy bear

Make sure young children follow a few rules for treating their pets properly:

1. The child's toy is taboo for the dog, and the reverse is equally true.

2. Children should not walk a dog on the leash until they are physically able to restrain him and can safely deal with difficult situations; for example, they know not to intervene if two dogs get into a fight.

3. Children and dogs should never romp around and roughhouse without supervision, and they should never get too wild; that way, high spirits will never lead them to overstep their bounds.

The behavior of children at play is definitely stressful for a dog, for example, when a child keeps shouting the dog's name, hands out rewards indiscriminately, or orders the dog around.

Wanted: Assistant coach

"Avoid frustration—strengthen team spirit" is the motto here. From about the age of five, children can be included in a game or exercise with the dog, and in the process you can clearly explain the dog's reactions.

28

For example, your little "assistant coach" can hide the treats in the box (❯ page 19). Many dog training schools offer classes for families with children age seven and up, where children learn things like how to understand the language of dogs.

Attend dog training classes together

Children who have a real interest in their dogs can try out a simple game or a little exercise on their own when they are a bit older (ages eight to ten). What works best is an exercise that you have rehearsed with the dog yourself and for which the dog—and the child—know the steps and the signals. Keep an eye on things so that you can intervene, if necessary, in case dog and child are still not on the same wavelength. Responsible adolescents can work independently with a dog. For many, it's fun to attend a training class together or participate in a sport with the dog (❯ from page 106).

Children and dogs get along with each other quite well when they respect each other. Adult guidance is necessary here: Explain to the child about the dog's nature and needs, for example, that the dog does not like to be touched when he's eating but would rather be left in peace. Also important: Family dogs need a place where they can retreat and not be disturbed by anybody. Even young children can learn this.

Many canine sports clubs or dog schools offer special courses for young people who would like to participate in activities with their four-legged friends. Practicing tricks together is not only fun, but it also strengthens the bond between them.

29

Searching and Fetching Games for Super Sleuths

One of the most fascinating traits of our four-legged friends is their superb sense of smell. The dog's ability to detect certain substances is a million times more acute than ours. No wonder we make use of this marvelous skill in critical areas like search and rescue, medicine, police work, and even military combat. For the dog, his "supernose" has to perform many tasks that were originally necessary for his survival. From tracking prey to locating water, he sniffs out everything that he needs to live, and to some degree even communication with other dogs depends on his olfactory cells.

Although most dogs are true geniuses at detecting scents, this ability must be trained if it is to be used for a specific purpose. Consequently, it makes sense to introduce "nose work" step by step, starting with small tasks like a simple Treasure Hunt (❯ pages 31 to 35). The dog's willingness to bring back the desired article is another training task that often poses a considerable challenge for both dog and owner, yet regular practice pays off. Games of searching and fetching are an excellent way to strengthen the bond between you and your four-legged friend—to say nothing of being great fun.

Treasure Hunt Indoors

 What this trains: In familiar surroundings, the dog learns to concentrate on searching for an article and giving it back willingly.

What you need: An article to hide (toy, scarf), leash and harness, and treats.

You can always delight your dog with this little game of hide-and-seek—and it doesn't take much time. Your four-legged friend has to look for a toy, a scarf, or some other article. Use only things that are reserved for playing with the dog. Even puppies quickly understand what this game is all about. The little ones won't be overtaxed if you design the game correctly and start out by playing it in a small area.

First a little test . . .

This game requires the dog to bring back the article she has found and give it to you. If you are not sure whether she'll really do this, try the following: Throw a toy a short distance away and tempt your dog to come to you as soon as she picks it up. If she brings it, take it from her while praising her and then give her a reward. If it doesn't work at first, take hold of the dog's harness and throw the toy no more than a leash-length away. The dog will run after it happily and pick it up. Now back up and pull the dog slowly toward you—she will follow. Praise her for it.

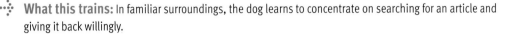

≫ EXPERT TIP

Adapt the training steps

Don't get irritated if something doesn't go smoothly right way. If a step in a game doesn't work, first check to see if it was an oversight on the dog's part, by trying the step again. If she makes the same mistake, ignore it and take a little break. For the dog to learn, it is important that she not make mistakes too often—otherwise they become ingrained in her behavior. Give some thought to what's causing the misunderstanding and how you could teach the step to the dog differently. You may have to go back to an earlier step in the training.

Trade the toy for a treat. Once the dog has mastered bringing back the toy and giving it to you, practice having her sniff out the article from its hiding place.

To do this, place the toy where the dog can see it, for example, behind a piece of furniture, a door jamb, or a wastepaper basket. Your dog waits quietly a few steps away. If she has mastered the *stay* command, you can use it for this purpose, or you can put her in the *sit* position.

Send your dog to search

After you have hidden the scarf or toy, go back to your dog and give her a signal to search for it. Now, she can find the toy and bring it back to you.

If everything goes according to plan, give her lots of praise and, naturally, a little reward in the form of a treat or a few minutes of free play (❯ Praising and rewarding, page 46).

Two or three rounds of this game are enough, then put the toy away again. Pros can even wait outside the door while you hide the article. That makes the task harder and more exciting.

Increase the distance

The next time, increase the distance a bit until that goes smoothly, too. Always make sure that the dog actually brings the article back to you again.

If she tears through the house with it instead, it's best if you go back to an earlier training step until your dog gives up her prey reliably. Otherwise, a mistake like this quickly becomes imprinted in her memory and it becomes very difficult to correct it in the future (❯ Expert tip, page 31).

1. Small distance: Although Monokel is an experienced ten-year-old Dalmatian, she is not familiar with this indoor game of hide-and-seek. Therefore, her owner starts by teaching her the game in small steps. Monokel sits nicely while her owner hides her scarf behind a wastepaper basket.

2. Master helps: Now her owner releases the *sit* command and lets Monokel find the scarf. Even without his assistance, the dog would certainly have found it.

3. Well spotted: Now it gets more difficult. The scarf is behind the sofa and the distance is somewhat greater. The owner sends his Dalmatian to look for it. Important: Don't watch the dog during the search; instead, look in the direction of the hiding place so that your four-legged friend follows your gaze.

4. Advanced level: Monokel has mastered bringing back an article and giving it up. Once this game goes smoothly, you can also have the dog wait outside the door to the room and then search, or else you can have the dog wait in one room while you hide the article in another room.

Treasure Hunt Outdoors

What this trains: During a treasure hunt, the most important thing is the ability to pay attention.

What you need: An article (cap, scarf, or glove) that you have reserved for walks with your dog and that can be left on the ground.

Dogs love a little variety in their walks. You can provide it, even when you're taking the usual route that you both already know by heart.

Making walks interesting

You can use a treasure hunt to focus your dog's attention fully on walking with you. His task is to find and indicate articles that you have lost along the path without letting the dog notice. The next time you take your dog for a walk, bring along a few articles, for example, a handkerchief, a cap, or a scarf. Lose them discreetly along the way. Turn around a bit later and retrace your route, the dog by your side. If he still can't manage to walk beside

you without a leash, you should put his leash on for the Treasure Hunt.

Something's lying there . . .

A slow walking pace is helpful in the beginning, so that the dog has enough time to discover the treasure. If he sniffs at it, pick up the article and make a big fuss over him for finding this wonderful object. Praise and reward him. If he runs past it without any reaction, turn around and walk so close to the cap, scarf, or handkerchief that the dog almost trips over it. If he notices the article now, praise him heartily and reward him. Then, go on to the next treasure. If he still doesn't react, find the article and make a big fuss over it. That makes the treasure attractive for your pet.

Pick up and give back

In the next step, your dog should pick up the article and give it to you. You can teach this with the clicker (❯ page 40). In the beginning, click at the first sign of every desired reaction, for example, when he doesn't just sniff at the article but also picks it up in his mouth. Once he does that a few times, wait until he holds on to it a moment longer before you click again. The dog will soon grasp what he has to do.

1. Treasure lost: The owner walks along a path with Marosch, her male Romanian Sheepdog, and discreetly loses a scarf and cap.

2. Treasure found: After losing the last article, the owner turns around. Even from a distance, Marosch has spotted the cap. The owner can rely on Marosch to walk by her side, so she doesn't need a leash for the Treasure Hunt.

3. Treasure delivered: The sheepdog quickly discovered the scarf, too, and even picked it up. The owner expresses her delight and immediately pulls out a treat.

35

Retrieving

What this trains: Most dogs love to retrieve things, and they really concentrate when they play this game. By using a variety of tasks, such as bringing back articles consistently, you can train obedience at the same time.

What you need: Something to throw, for example, a toy or a ball; treats as rewards.

For most dogs, chasing after things is in their blood—they love it! Many think there's nothing better than retrieving an article, be it a ball, a favorite toy, or a retrieving "bumper." However, not all dogs are equally enthusiastic when their owner wants them to bring back their prey, too. And besides, a dog would much rather race after an object as it flies through the air.

Stop! Our game begins here. Of course, the dog should run after the object you've thrown, but not until you give her the signal.

Tip: Don't throw pointed sticks, because they could injure the dog.

Getting ready for the game

A classic game might look like this: You have the dog sit while you stand next to her and throw one of her toys far away. You curb the dog's impulse to race off immediately in pursuit, perhaps with the *stay* signal. Only after a few moments do you allow her to run toward the article, using a signal that you have chosen for retrieving, for example, "Bring it back!"

You can also reinforce the signal with a gesture, for example, opening your arms in front of you (❯ photo, page 37).

Bringing it back

Naturally, you would like the dog to bring back to you what you've thrown. If she doesn't do that on her own, run away from her and squat down. She will now follow you with the toy in her mouth. If she comes to you, praise her enthusiastically and take the toy away from her—in the beginning, in exchange for something else, perhaps a treat. If this version works well, get more demanding: Introduce a little exercise before the *bring* signal, for example, "Weave Through My Legs" (❯ pages 56/57) or a *down*. You and your pet can also work on this game indoors.

For pros: Before the *bring* signal, change your position. Call the dog over to you and give her a little task. Only then do you send her off.

1. Wait patiently: The owner has Gina, her female Golden Retriever, sit next to her and gives her the command *"Stay!"* (❯ photo, page 36).

2. Throw the toy: Gina's favorite toy flies through the air. The dog doesn't run after it right away, but instead remains sitting nicely.

3. Wait a moment: The owner waits briefly before she gives the signal to retrieve. At the same time, she makes eye contact with Gina.

4. Go get it: With clear body language, the owner gives her dog the command *"Bring it back!"* Gina would also understand her owner's request without the verbal signal.

5. Give it back: Well done! Gina brings her toy straight back to her owner and puts it in her outstretched hand. In the beginning, she was always rewarded with a treat for this, but now it's just occasionally.

Find the Treat Bag

 What this trains: The dog learns to concentrate on using her nose and to give back something that is very important for her, namely, her food. This exercise trains her sense of smell and obedience, because she has to pick up the prey at a signal and give it back again.

What you need: Leash (or long line) and harness, treat bag (or a small pouch), and treats.

This exciting game could become a perennial favorite for you and your dog. All dogs have a lot of fun searching for something, especially when tempted by a tasty reward.

Make the prey interesting

In the beginning, take the dog by the harness and leash. Then make the treat-filled bag attractive: Throw it up in the air or drag it back and forth on the ground. You can also encourage your dog to play a little game of tug-of-war with it. Reward your dog from the treat bag.

Reward every little success

Once you've piqued your dog's interest in the bag, toss it a short distance away. The dog is now allowed to run after it. If all goes well, she'll pick it up. Praise her enthusiastically and walk backward. When you do that, the dog automatically has to follow you on the leash. When she comes to you, praise her, take the bag away from her, and reward her from it. If necessary, pull the dog gently toward you.

Once the dog is picking up the bag and bringing it back reliably, you can begin the first small search without the leash; introduce the verbal and visual signals in the process (for example, *"Fetch!"* and a suitable arm motion). First, make the treat bag attractive for the dog again. Then have her *sit*. Now place the bag about five yards (5 m) away, slightly hidden. After you give the signal, the dog may begin to search. Once she finds the bag, make a big fuss over her and reward her from it as soon as she brings it to you. In case she's having trouble bringing it back to you, repeat the exercise with the long line. Give the dog time to search, and don't keep repeating the signal. Only if you have the feeling that the dog is wandering around aimlessly should you call her to you and send her off again in the direction of the treat bag. Now, you can gradually increase the distance when you hide the bag. The dog should be successful every time she searches!

For proficient super sleuths: Don't allow the dog to watch when you hide the bag, but start off with shorter distances.

1. Practice patience: Alex recognizes her treat bag. She has mastered searching and fetching with the leash. Today she and her owner are going to practice without a leash. Alex is permitted to watch the preparations in the *sit* position.

2. Lay down the bag: The owner lays the bag on the ground about five to ten yards (5 to 10 m) away, but still within view of Alex. Alex can hardly wait for the game to begin.

3. **Out of sight:** The owner increases the level of difficulty. The five-year-old Golden Retriever can only see approximately where the bag is hidden. Nevertheless, she remains patiently in the *sit* position, as she has learned to do.

4. **Without a word:** After hiding the bag, the owner returns to her dog and gives her a signal to begin the search. At the same time, the owner looks in the direction of the treat bag.

5. **Found and brought back:** Alex receives her well-deserved reward directly from the treat bag. Her owner didn't walk along with her on the search, but waited patiently back at the starting point.

Clicker Training

The clicker makes a noise like a metal frog toy when you squeeze it. It is an ideal training aid when you want to teach the dog something.

Give a click as soon as the dog performs the desired action. The great thing about it: This is followed immediately by a food reward. In canine learning theory, this is called "positive reinforcement" and "operant conditioning." The dog makes the connection between the sound/reward and his own actions and, after enough repetitions, stores them in his behavioral repertoire.

Why a click?

Naturally, you can also acknowledge your dog with words, but it's no easy matter to give a verbal signal like *"Well done!"* in a split second at precisely the right moment. With a clicker, you can acknowledge the correct behavior very precisely once you get the timing right. That means you have to watch your dog carefully in order to click at the exact moment he shows the desired behavior. A short, sharp click often makes more of an impression on the dog than a *"Well done!"* Theoretically, instead of a clicker you could also use a very short word that you speak in a similar snappy manner, like *"Yay!"* or *"Yip!"*

The first step

First, you have to condition the dog to the clicker: Stand facing your dog with the clicker in your hand. Click once and immediately give him a treat. Repeat this four or five times at intervals through-out the day. As soon as the dog responds attentively to a click, he has figured out that the sound means a reward for him. From now on, you can use the

Ginger under-stands: At the click, she looks up attentively. Now that she has made the connection between the sound and a food reward, it can be used when training her in the future. Conditioning is the first step. Important: Always click just once, not several times. And never use the clicker for any other purpose, for instance, to call the dog to you. It is only intended for positive reinforcement.

clicker as a positive reinforcer. An example: You would like to teach your puppy, young dog, or adult dog that he should go to his blanket on your signal. Watch your dog when he is near the blanket. If he happens to put a paw on the blanket, click once and immediately give him a treat. Don't tempt him to step on the blanket, but wait until he does it accidentally.

Repeat this a few times until you're sure the dog has made the connection between stepping on the blanket and the click (and a reward). Now raise the bar: The dog has to put two paws on the blanket. If he steps on it with just one paw, wait until the

second paw follows, then click and treat. Practice
that until the dog is standing with all four paws on
the blanket. Soon you can introduce a verbal signal
for it: The moment the dog puts all four paws on
the blanket, you say, *"Go to your blanket!"* and
click—don't forget the treat. So that the dog learns
to stay on his blanket longer, gradually delay giving
the click—one minute at first, then two, and so on.
This way, you increase the length of time he stays
there. Eventually the dog will grasp the meaning of
the signal even without clicker. Then, continue to
praise him with just your voice and give him a treat
now and then—until you can phase that out, too.
Although it sounds simple, clicker training requires
an understanding of some basic principles.
There are training manuals on the subject
(❯ page 189), and many dog training
schools now offer clicker training, too.

Ginger is being
conditioned to a target stick
with the help of the clicker. The
goal is for her to follow the stick with
her nose (and later with her paw), so
that she can be guided in any direction.
Her owner holds the stick in her hand and
waits patiently until Ginger happens to
sniff at it—click and reward. Once Ginger
has made the connection, she can
even be taught to touch just the
end of the stick with her nose
(or paw).

Little by little, the
four-month-old female is
learning to go onto her doggy
blanket. At first, her owner clicks
whenever Ginger happens to put
a paw on the blanket. Later, her
owner only clicks when it's two
paws—until finally Ginger is
standing on the blanket with
all four paws.

41

Find the Scented Towel

 What this trains: This game is an excellent way to put your dog's nose to the test. If her talent for scenting is still dormant, it will teach her to concentrate when using her sense of smell.

What you need: A cloth towel; a scent, with, honey dissolved in water, or milk (no perfumes or essential oils); several paper towels; and possibly a clicker (❯ page 40).

Even a tiny drop of scent on a paper towel is enough for the dog to distinguish it from other unscented towels.

The scent test

First, familiarize your dog with the scent that you want to use for this game. Put a few drops of it on a cloth towel; then, you and the dog play with the towel. After this preparation, it's on to the nose work. Prepare a paper towel with the scent and place it on the floor in front of the dog. Allow the dog to give it a good sniff. Now, your reaction is important: Act as if the dog has just found some

long-lost treasure, pick up the towel, smell it, and make a big fuss over it. Now, try the whole thing with two towels, one with a drop of scent and the other without. Let the dog smell both towels. Praise her enthusiastically if she reacts a moment longer to the correct towel, for example, if she sniffs at it or picks it up. After a few repetitions, the dog will probably grasp that she is supposed to find the scent. If she doesn't understand this yet or if she repeatedly shreds the towels, resort to a little trick: Put each towel in the bottom of a narrow, empty jelly jar or a tall drinking glass.

Find the scented towel, step by step

Watch how your dog indicates the correct scent: Does she pick up the towel? Does she touch it with her paw? Or does she simply pause longer by the right towel? You can reinforce her "indicator behavior" with the clicker.

You shouldn't try to teach this game in just one day. Give the dog plenty of time for the individual steps. Meanwhile, keep practicing. For super sleuths that have no trouble recognizing the correct scent, put out more towels, only one of which is scented. To make it even harder, take a new scent, let your dog smell it before the start of the game, and challenge her to sniff out the towel with this scent from among two or three that you have laid out.

1. **Scented Towel:** The hand towel in the photo on page 42 was prepared with honey dissolved in water. Amy was allowed to play with it so that she would become familiar with the scent. For the actual nose work, a paper towel is moistened with the same scent.

2. **Tricky business:** Amy is supposed to fetch the towel with the correct scent. It works perfectly with two towels—but with three?

3. **No problem:** Amy goes straight to the paper towel with diluted honey. Her nose has shown her the way. As she sniffs at it, her owner praises her. She brings it back to her owner and gets a click and a tasty treat in return.

43

Lost and Found

 What this trains: Your dog learns to pay close attention to you and, on her own, to indicate an article that you have lost. She uses her sense of smell when you send her to search for the article.

What you need: Leash, an article of yours that the dog can pick up easily (for example, your eyeglass case or key wallet), and treats.

The dog should notice on her own that you have lost something and indicate it, for instance, by sitting near the article.

Make a big fuss over the find

To teach this game, leash the dog and take her for a walk along a path. As you're walking, lose something, for example, an (empty) eyeglass case—and make sure the dog notices as you do it. If she sniffs at the article, pick it up, make a big fuss over it, and then praise the dog and reward her. If the dog does not react to the lost object but instead simply keeps on walking with you, turn back after a few steps.

Pass so close to the article that the dog almost trips over it. If she notices the article now, show how pleased you are, as described above, praise her, and reward her.

You lost something there . . .

Now the dog walks along with you off-leash and has to learn to stay by the article in order to indicate that you have lost something. After you have lost the article, continue walking and watch the dog out of the corner of your eye. As soon as she hesitates even slightly near the article, turn around immediately, praise her, and make a big fuss over the find again. Don't forget the reward!

If that works well, the next time wait a little longer before turning around and returning to your dog and her find. This way, she'll gradually learn that she is supposed to remain by the lost article. Waiting pays off: When you return to her, make a huge fuss over the find and reward her again.

A variant for advanced students: Lose an object discreetly so that the dog really doesn't notice it. A few steps later, discover your loss and send the dog back to retrieve the lost article, for example, with the signal *"Fetch!"*

1. On-leash: The owner has lost a red eyeglass case along the path. Her female dog Turbo sniffs at it. The owner reacts immediately with praise and makes a big fuss over Turbo's find.

2. Off-leash: In the second step, the owner and Turbo practice having the dog indicate the loss of the article on her own. To do this, the owner walks a little further after losing the article. Turbo sits next to the case and in this way attracts her owner's attention to the lost object.

3. "Fetch what I've lost!": This time Turbo's owner has lost something without letting the dog notice it. A few yards later, the owner sends her dog back to search for the article using a verbal signal and a gesture.

4. Found: Turbo has run back along the path and discovered the article. The dog picks up the red eyeglass case and brings it back to the owner.

5. Retrieved: Turbo gets lots of praise and, naturally, a reward for bringing back the case. To make this exercise more difficult, you can increase the distance.

Praising and Rewarding Correctly

The right praise at the right time along with a tasty reward will make every dog an enthusiastic teammate.

Show that you're genuinely pleased

Your dog can easily tell the difference between a lukewarm "Good job" and an enthusiastic "Wow! That was great!" So praise him like you mean it. Verbal fireworks are in order, especially when your companion has mastered a task for the first time.

A short word for praise

A short, high-pitched *"Great!"* or *"Yay!"* acknowledges a correct action on the spot, for example, when you practice individual steps in a game like "Find the Treat Bag" on page 38. A word of praise like this can also serve as a substitute for the clicker (❯ page 40). Don't forget the food reward afterward.

Treats and play as rewards

It's best to reward food-oriented types with tasty treats, but for dogs that are less fixated on food, a few minutes of play is better. Try it yourself and possibly combine the two. Tip: Always give a treat when you would like to reward something on the spot, for example, a simple *sit*. A short, exciting game with a ball or rope makes an ideal reward for a series of actions (for example, after a well-executed "Weave Through My Legs," pages 56/57) or after an active game (like agility).

No petting, please

Many dogs don't like it when someone pets them during a game or an exercise. How can you tell? Your dog looks away, turns his head aside, and puts his ears back. The reason may be that a touch, even if it is well intentioned, distracts him from the task

Tasty treats as a reward are simply tops for most dogs. Be careful, though, that your four-legged friend takes the treat calmly rather than snatching it greedily from your hand. To prevent food rewards from spoiling his figure, it's best to use only small treats. Always deduct the treats from your dog's daily food ration.

at hand. Male dogs often seem more irritated than females by stroking rewards during training.

Praise and reward immediately

If your dog does something right, praise and reward him immediately, because that's the only way he will associate the reward with the action he just performed. That's also why clicker training (❯ page 40) can be used so successfully in many exercises (or else a suitably brief word of praise like *"Yay!"* as a substitute for the clicker).

Variety and jackpot

Vary the food reward; occasionally you could give especially yummy treats like cheese, dried fish, or cooked bits of chicken. Small pieces usually suffice. A truly fantastic performance calls for the jackpot: Much more of a good thing, a regular handful.

Praise for pros

Your dog should obey routine commands like *sit* or *down* without regular food rewards (but always with verbal praise!). Even here, though, a tasty treat now and then keeps him motivated to perform well. Everything that is outside the daily repertoire or that you are training always deserves a reward.

Cuddling is a wonderful thing for many dogs (and for their owners, too). However, it's important to choose the right moment for it. Most dogs don't like to be petted during a game—it ruins their concentration. Later on, though, they may be all the more happy to have a relaxing moment together, once the training is over and it's time for a cuddle.

It doesn't always have to be a treat: A game of tug-of-war is also a great reward. Free play is an ideal way to reduce tension, especially if your dog had to concentrate on a task or a game longer than usual.

47

Scent Trail

What this trains: Every dog has an amazing sense of smell. However, he has to learn how to concentrate on following a specific scent trail. Here you can use a game to teach him how to do it while encouraging him to work independently.

What you need: A harness, a leash, and two articles to indicate the beginning and the end of the track; for example, a glove and a bunch of keys.

If your dog has had no experience with tracking, he'll definitely develop a taste for it with this game.

Laying the track

Start with a simple track, ideally one in fairly high grass. Indicate the beginning with one article. From there, walk straight ahead, scuffing your feet to make a swath of scented track about two feet wide. Continue laying the track in this manner for about 20 to 30 feet (7 to 10 m), and, at the end of the track, set down the other article. Then, take a giant step away from the track and circle back to your dog.

Always use leash and harness

Take your dog to the starting point of the track. Let him sniff at the article you have placed there. Use a command reserved for tracking—like *"Track!"* or *"Find!"*—to have your dog follow the scent. To help him get started, put your hand on the ground to show him where the track begins. As soon as he has picked up the scent, he will follow it with his nose. Walk behind him, keeping a little tension on the leash. If the dog strays from the track, wait a moment to see if he finds his way back on his own. If he doesn't, help him by indicating the track with your hand. You can repeat the signal at this point, but don't do it too often. As soon as the dog reaches the article, make a big fuss over his find. Praise him enthusiastically and reward him, even if you gave him a lot of help. Once you have practiced this initial tracking exercise three or four times, you can be more demanding. Don't scuff your feet when you lay the track; instead, walk on ahead normally. Increase the length of the track and include one and, later, several changes of direction. Pros can even sniff their way along a circular track. It is important to take your time training every new challenge until your dog has mastered it. Leading the dog correctly is also important; you'll find what that involves under "Tracking" on pages 148/149.

1. Lay the track: Scuffing her feet, the owner lays a track. It's best to start by simply walking in a straight line for about 20 to 30 feet (7 to 10 m). For beginners, tracks in high grass are ideal because they are easier to follow.

2. Leave the track: The owner takes a giant step away from the track so that her scent ends here. She marks the end of the track with an article. Then she circles back to her dog.

3. Picking up the scent: A leash and harness are always used for tracking. Rossini is allowed to sniff the first scent article once more, then he's off.

4. Following the scent: With his nose to the ground, the dog follows his owner's scent and sniffs along the track she left. If he wanders off the track, his owner waits a while to see if he finds it again on his own. If he doesn't, she uses her hand to show him where it continues.

5. The end of the trail: When Rossini reaches the article at the finish line, his owner makes a big fuss over her super sleuth and praises him enthusiastically. She also gives him a tasty reward from her treat bag.

Find the **Missing Person**

 What this trains: Here the dog leans to use his sense of smell to find a person and to concentrate on following a trail. This game builds on the "Scent Trail" ❯ page 48.

What you need: A harness, a leash, another person, an article belonging to this person, and clothespins or colored ties to mark the trail in the field.

Now things get even more exciting for super sleuths! The dog is not following just a track, but the trail of a stranger whose scent he has picked up. It's best if he doesn't search for his owner, because many dogs get nervous and have trouble concentrating when they lose sight of their owner.

Colored clothespins show the way

Like all tracking, this is done with a leash and harness. It is a continuation of the "Scent Trail" game (❯ page 48). The stranger (who can be someone the dog knows) starts by laying a track about 20 to 30 yards (20 to 30 m) long, marking the route with colored clothespins or ties so that it will be possible to tell later whether or not the dog is actually following the track. While this is going on, tether your dog securely so that he can't watch these activities. The stranger hides at the end of the track, perhaps behind a tree (where the dog won't be able to see him/her).

Give the signal to start

For an inexperienced dog, lay the article belonging to the missing person at the beginning of the track. Later, the dog can just be allowed to sniff at the article, and then he has to find the track for himself. But first lead your dog to the start of the track and have him *sit*. Let him smell the article. Then give the signal for him to start searching, for example, *"Track!"* or *"Find!"* The dog begins to follow the track. If he doesn't have the faintest idea what to do, indicate a small stretch of the track with your hand. Once he is finally on the trail, if he wanders off from time to time (or tries to pick up the scent by sniffing the air), remain standing and wait to see if he returns to the trail on his own. If he doesn't, help him find it again by pointing to the track. The dog should be able to take his time using his nose, so be patient and don't repeat the signal too often. While your dog sniffs his way forward, walk behind him. If he finds the person, reward him.

1. Mark the track: An acquaintance stranger marks the track with colored clothespins, putting them high enough above the ground that the dog won't be able to spot them.

2. Check the scent: Henry the Labrador is already an experienced tracker. That's why he no longer needs to have someone show him where the track begins; instead, the handler lets him sniff a scarf belonging to the missing person.

3. On the track: While Henry follows the track, his owner, runs along behind him, holding the tracking leash loosely in her hand.

4. Help when needed: If Henry strays from the track, his owner gives him a little time to pick up the scent again. If he's having trouble, she gives him some help.

5. Missing person found: Henry has discovered the acquaintance (stranger) is hiding behind a tree trunk. She praises Henry and rewards him from the treat bag.

Active Games to Stay in Shape

Running, romping, jumping – most dogs love this more than anything. It satisfies the craving for activity they inherited from their ancestor, the wolf—who, after all, is a cursorial animal, adapted for running.

When hunting for food, wolves can travel distances of 12 to 30 miles (20 to 50 km) in a night at an easy trot. Domestic dogs today rarely get the opportunity to indulge their love of running to such an extent.

Then, there are breed-specific differences that have been developed over the centuries: A Basset Hound would be much less enthusiastic about the wolf's way of life than, for example, a Siberian Husky, for whom distance and speed are everything.

For both types—and for the enormous range between—active games are ideal if they are tailored to the individual needs, age, and condition of the dog.

The games on the following pages focus sometimes on speed, like "Dog Racing" on page 58; sometimes on agility, like "Weave Through My Legs" on page 56; or sometimes on correctly following directions, like "Mountain Climbing" on page 60. Your job: Experiment to find out what your dog really enjoys and which games provide the right outlet for his need for activity.

Go Around the **Obstacle**

What this trains: The dog learns to walk around an obstacle (post, tree, or bush) at your signal and then come back to you. To do this, he has to concentrate on you in order to interpret specific signals correctly.

What you need: Possibly a leash for the first attempt, treats as a reward, and an obstacle to go around.

Say good-bye to boredom on your daily walks! This game makes every walk an adventure. It is also a great way to help rambling dogs concentrate a bit more on their master. And the better your four-legged friend gets at walking around an obstacle, the more challenging you can make the game.

The first lesson

The dog has to understand what it means to walk around an obstacle. If your dog is still uncertain and stays next to you, take him on the leash for the first exercise.

Position yourself and your dog one step away from an obstacle, for example, a post or a small tree. If your dog is on your left side, take a treat in your right hand. Now with your left hand, guide your dog around the obstacle. When you can see him on the other side, back up a step or two—the dog will follow you. Reward him with the treat from your right hand. Once the dog understands what to do, you can introduce the command for it, for example, *"Go around left!"* The correct sequence of events finally looks like this: The dog stands or sits at your left side, looking at the obstacle. Standing erect, you send him around the obstacle with a gesture of your left arm (while you remain at your position) and reward the dog from your right hand when he reaches you.

Increase the distance

As soon as the dog goes around the obstacle reliably, increase the distance in very small stages. To do this, you should be able to practice with the dog off-leash. Be careful not to demand too much of him, though—every little step away from the obstacle is quite a big achievement for your dog, so teach the exercise slowly, step by step!

Once the dog is comfortable going around the object on one side, practice the other side, too. That might not be for a few weeks, depending on how intensively you train and how quickly your dog takes to the game.

Increase the degree of difficulty

Once your dog can circle the obstacle from both sides and is doing it reliably, you can devise all sorts of variations. For the dog, it is a real challenge if you

have him circle a fairly large tree or even a bush that he can't see around. To make sure that it works right away here, too, start by decreasing the distance again for each new obstacle until the dog can handle this more difficult task without any problems.

If your dog has mastered going around obstacles, think up new challenges for him. For example, after your dog circles the obstacle, you can give him the command to *stop* or *stay* (assuming he knows this signal) and make him wait until you release the command before continuing. Even an occasional *sit* or *down* is a new challenge. Or you can have him stop right behind the obstacle and then send him back around it in the opposite direction using

gestures and voice commands. With a pro, you can even train him to go around a group of trees or walk a figure eight between two trees. This game is ideal on walks, because there are almost endless possibilities for varying and elaborating on it. In the park, for example, you can have your dog go around a fountain, a bench, or a little pond. It's also possible to practice this game with your dog indoors. That makes you independent of wind and weather. Suitable obstacles here could be a chair that you place in the middle of the room or a table, if there is enough room to move around it. Even a large houseplant will do. As you can see, there are no limits to your imagination.

1. Object found: A lone tree like this one invites you to *go around*. The owner has called her mixed-breed dog Joey over to her and had him *sit* at her left.

2. Off you go!: The owner sends Joey on his way with gestures and voice commands. Joey has to go around the tree clockwise and then come back to her again.

3. Not an easy task: From this distance, the task takes real skill. The dog has practiced circling on many walks and has it down pat. Nevertheless, he gets a reward each time he does it perfectly.

4. Take two: Now both dogs are supposed to go around the tree in opposite directions. Using voice and arm signals, the owner sends the two on their way.

5. High expectations: Lola is supposed to go around Joey. That requires a lot of concentration and discipline, because they are not allowed to sniff each other and have to tolerate being near the other dog. This version is only suitable for dogs that know and like each other.

Weave Through My Legs

 What this trains: What's important here is agility—and really good teamwork! That's because dog and owner move in unison, but each one plays a different role.

What you need: Treats, and athletic apparel (skirts, dresses, or long coats are not suitable).

This game will lift your spirits! Most dogs learn it very quickly, if you don't demand too much from them right away.

A treat in each hand

Here's what you have to do: Walk slowly forward taking big steps (later you can do it faster); at a hand signal from you, your dogs walks along, weaving through your legs. To do this, start by placing the dog at your side so that he is standing with his shoulder parallel to your knee. Hold a treat in each hand. If the dog is standing at your right side, take a big step forward with your left leg and lure the dog through your legs with the treat in your left hand.

As he walks through, praise him. Don't give him the treat until he is standing parallel to your left leg— then start the next step. This is important so that the dog doesn't stop the weave too soon. Then follow the same procedure starting from the left: Move the right leg forward and lure the dog through with the treat in your right hand.

Slowly increase the degree of difficulty

Repeat the exercise two or three times until your dog understands how to move. Then, you can gradually increase the length of the weave. At this point, don't give a treat for every individual step of the weave, but instead wait until you have completed a short series of steps. Stop practicing, though, before the dog begins to lose interest.

Now start phasing out the treats. To do this, give a clear visual signal: If the dog is supposed to walk through your legs from left to right, show him the direction using your left hand (❯ photo 4, page 57) and give him the reward with your right hand. If that goes well, leave the treat in your pocket the next time. The dog doesn't get it until he has completed the weave chain. This way, you get a fluid weave. Naturally, a well-coordinated team can practice the whole thing backward, too—but starting again, step by step.

1. The lure of the treat: The owner started with her mixed-breed dog Toni on the right side. After taking one big step with her left leg, she lures him through her legs with a treat in her left hand.

2. A well-deserved reward: Toni doesn't get the treat until he is parallel to his owner's left leg again. This way she teaches Toni to execute the weave correctly from start to finish, because now he is in position to begin the next step of the weave.

3. At the hand signal: Now the owner's can almost stand up straight as she walks forward. She merely gives Toni a hand signal to indicate the direction. At this point, he doesn't get a treat until he finishes a series of weaves.

4. For experts: A hand signal from the owner is all it takes, and Toni weaves through his owner's legs for the whole distance.

Dog Racing

 What this trains: Concentration and discipline are put to the test here, because the dog has to wait for a signal before he starts to run, and he is not allowed to chase after the other dog.

What you need: A partner with a dog—the two dogs should know each other and get along well—and treats to reward the dogs.

Taking a walk with another dog owner is always a nice change of pace, and it's the perfect opportunity for a game together. Speed is not what matters most in this game, but rather it's the ability of your four-legged teammate to wait patiently until it's his turn! This entertaining game requires that your dog has mastered the *stay* signal, because in the beginning only one of the two runners is called to run at a time. The other one has to remain sitting at the starting line until he finally gets the signal to run.

Begin practicing one at a time . . .

First, have your dog practice waiting patiently. To do this, have him *sit* while you move away a bit, then go back to him and praise him for waiting patiently. Next, train the recall, starting with a short distance. Have him *sit* and then give him the signal to *stay*. Move only a few steps away, stand facing him, and call him to you with an encouraging tone of voice. Praise him lavishly when he reaches you, and reward him.

. . . then practice with two at once

Once that works well, you and your partner can lead both dogs to the starting point and give each of them the *stay* signal. In the beginning, move only a few steps away, then turn around and face the dogs. Agree beforehand whose dog will be called first. If it works right away—one dog races toward his owner while the other sits patiently—then both dogs deserve a big helping of praise! If a dog is having trouble waiting patiently at the starting point, lead the early starter silently but kindly back to the start and begin the game again—this time with a shorter distance. If the dog manages to wait this time, go up to him and reward him. Now you can gradually increase the distance. For the final round, let both dogs start at the same time—and here speed counts!

1. Starting position: Amy and Jumping Sioux have already mastered the *stay* signal. They look expectantly at their owners and wait for the signal to begin.

2. Ladies first: Amy is allowed to start first. The treat bag in her owner's hand adds to the pleasure of running straight to her. Once there, she gets a reward from it. Meanwhile, Sioux continues to sit patiently.

3. Now it's Sioux's turn: Amy's owner has brought her back to the starting point, and now it's finally Sioux's turn. His owner calls his Nova Scotia Duck Tolling Retriever, and this time Amy has to *sit* and *stay*—quite an impressive achievement at this distance.

4. The race: Now they finish with a little race. Both dogs wait patiently until they get the signal to start—this time both at once. The two dogs make a dash for their owners.

"Mountain Climbing" Made Easy

What this trains: The dog learns to concentrate, follow directions independently, and carry out commands at a distance.

What you need: A small embankment and treats.

This is a great way to practice concentration when you're out walking with your dog, and it's ideal if your dog tends to forget that she's not taking a walk all by herself.

Start with a little hill

First, the dog learns to let you send her off in a specific direction. To do this, find a small embankment and stand at the bottom of it with your dog. Now send your dog up the slope with an arm motion and a verbal signal, for example, *"Up!"* If the dog takes only one or two steps up the hill and then stops, the embankment is still too high. Find a lower one, if necessary, one where it only takes

the dog two steps to reach the top. Praise the dog when she succeeds and reward her with a treat right away. Then call the dog to you again, using your customary signal—reward this, too. Now send her up the mini-hill one or two more times. That's enough to start with. In the next step, you can practice having your dog carry out simple commands at the top of the hill, for example *sit* or *down*. Praise her enthusiastically each time, of course, then call her back to you again.

It gets tricky up on top

As the height of the slope increases, so do the challenges for your dog. That's why you should always go up in small stages: Be on the lookout for a slightly higher hill and practice there. In order to make the task more attractive for the dog, you can even hide the treat bag at the top occasionally.

Once the dog does a good job being sent up the hill and returning to you, you can have her do something more challenging up on top, for example, a little trick that your dog has already mastered. Always end the exercise with a recall, which the dog should carry out correctly—only then do you continue with your walk. For advanced students, there are more difficult variations: For example, stop the dog as she runs up or back down a slope (one that's not too steep), and then have her continue on her way.

1. Up the hill: The owner sends Turbo up a steep embankment with a verbal signal and a gesture. This height is still too challenging for beginners, but Turbo knows this game and loves it.

2. Give a command: Up on top, Turbo carries out the command her owner gives her from below—at this distance, that's quite an accomplishment. The female sheepdog remains attentively in the *sit* position until the next signal comes.

Descent: After a few exercises up on top of the embankment, her owner calls Turbo back to her with a verbal command and clear gesture. Turbo charges happily downhill.

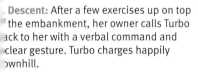

On we go: The dog also stops well on command as she goes up or down the hill. This exercise, though, is best left to experts. And now the owner and Turbo continue their walk.

61

Jump Through the Hoop

What this trains: If you make a game of it, even a puppy can be enticed to go through a hoop. In this introduction to sports equipment, the puppy learns how to coordinate his movements. For older dogs, this game is an excellent agility exercise.

What you need: Depending on the size of the dog, a small, medium, or large hula hoop.

Whether you have a puppy, a small breed, or a big dog, there's a hoop to fit every size. Tailor the difficulty of the exercise to the age and condition of your dog. Even a puppy can be enticed through a hoop if you make it fun; in the process, he learns to coordinate his movements. A puppy begins by climbing through the hoop; because his young bones are still developing, he should not be making big jumps yet (❯ Bicycling, pages 112/113). For healthy adult dogs, the more they like to jump, the higher they can go; always be careful, though— make sure you look before your dog leaps.

The first time let him sniff

Although the hoop looks perfectly safe to us humans, some dogs may find it frightening at first. Give your dog an opportunity to get used to this unfamiliar contraption. Without saying a word, lay the hoop in front of him on the ground. Sooner or later he will get curious, approach it, and sniff at it cautiously. However, if you put a treat in the middle of the hoop (or closer to the edge for very timid dogs), the whole business becomes more interesting.

Once the dog is used to the hoop, calmly hold it up in front of him and tempt him through it with a food reward. Once that has worked well several times, you can also introduce a verbal signal for it, for example, *"Through!"* or *"Hula hoop!"*

Soft ground beneath his paws

Increase the demands of the exercise very slowly. Gradually hold the hoop a little higher—for a young dog, keep it low enough that he doesn't have to jump very high. Make sure the dog always lands on soft ground. Dogs usually learn quickly how to jump through a hoop. They won't get bored, though, if you keep thinking up new variations.

Hoop jump with variations

For example, this one: First, have your dog *sit* patiently, before you give him the signal to jump through.

1. **Getting acquainted with the hoop:** Small dog, small hoop: For Monster, the little Yorkshire Terrier with the big name, this miniature hula hoop is just right. He was allowed to sniff at the hoop and now it doesn't scare him any more.

2. **The first run through:** The owner first has her little dog *sit* and then tempts him through the hoop with a treat. At the same time, she gives him the appropriate verbal signal. After a few test runs, Monster understands what this game is all about.

Then, you can slowly move away from the dog so that he has to run a short distance before he can make his jump. Don't forget the reward! Every increase in distance is a challenge. If it doesn't work, decrease the distance again. Don't try any little tricks to motivate the dog to jump higher. Quickly raising the hoop just before the dog jumps is absolutely taboo. He could get hurt! The hula hoop offers many possibilities for entertaining games: Lay two or three hoops on the ground and send your dog from one to another (❯ photo, page 12). In each hoop, have him carry out a command, for example, *sit* or *down*. Hoop games are excellent for children who have already learned how to practice little exercises with their dog.

3. **The first jump:** On soft ground, a jump of this height is easy for the Yorkie to handle. The owner holds the hoop far enough away from her body so that the dog has plenty of room to jump.

"Tree Touch"

What this trains: Here you teach the dog to go where you direct her and then carry out a specific action there.

What you need: A clicker (> page 40), a stick like the stakes used for backyard or balcony gardening, an obstacle to touch (here a tree), and treats.

You can fit this game in any time and any place—even indoors—as a little exercise in paying attention. At your signal, the dog touches an obstacle that you point out to her (here a tree). A prerequisite is that your dog is familiar with clicker training (> page 40).

Training with the target stick

Using a clicker, first teach your dog to touch a stick with her nose; in technical jargon, this is referred to as a "target stick." To do this, stand near your dog, hold the stick loosely in your hand, and wait until the dog sniffs at it inquisitively. Each time she sniffs

at the stick, click and give her a treat right away. Once the dog understands what she has to do, namely, to touch the stick, you can continue to shape her behavior using the clicker.

Next, the dog has to learn to touch only the tip of the stick. Click each time the dog touches the stick a little closer to the tip (don't forget the treats). Once she is consistently touching just the end of the stick with her nose, you can direct her anywhere easily and accurately. This is precisely the behavior we need for this game.

To the tree

In the next step, direct your dog to a tree using the target stick—after all, she has learned to follow the stick with her nose. Click when the dog touches a spot on the tree trunk that you indicate with the stick. After the dog understands what's expected of her, introduce a verbal signal, for example, *To the tree!* Once the dog internalizes the signal, she will touch the tree trunk even without the stick; give it a try.

If she can't manage it yet, go back to an earlier step in the exercise (> Expert tip, page 31). Eventually, you can train the signal from a distance. To do this, gradually move farther and farther from the tree until you can send the dog a distance of several yards. Take your time with this game.

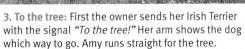

1. Practice touching: Amy follows the stick and touches the tree at the spot indicated by the tip of the stick. In return, she gets a click and a treat.

2. The excitement grows: The owner stands a few yards from the tree. She puts her dog in the *sit* position. Before she gives the verbal signal for the Tree Touch, she makes sure that Amy is looking at her attentively and eagerly.

3. To the tree: First the owner sends her Irish Terrier with the signal *"To the tree!"* Her arm shows the dog which way to go. Amy runs straight for the tree.

4. Mission accomplished: The dog touches the tree at the desired height, just the way she practiced earlier with the target stick and clicker.

Out in Public with **Your Dog**

How do you avoid stress and aggravation when you're out walking with your dog? It's really quite simple. With a little thoughtfulness and a few rules, games or walks with your dog will become a relaxed affair for everyone concerned.

1   **Dog poop:** Dog droppings belong in a poop bag—and then go into the nearest trash receptacle. You can get poop bags in pet stores (as well as online), and a growing number of cities and towns are putting up bag dispensers. Sometimes the trash cans are right next to them.

2   **Joggers, bicyclists, and children at play:** These figures have an almost magical attraction for many dogs! If it's like that for your dog, teach him to ignore these temptations, for example, with long line training (or, if necessary, with professional help).

3   **Uninvited playmates:** When you are playing a game with your dog out in public and another dog comes over to see what's going on, stop your game. This way, you will avoid potential wrangling over the toy and won't confront your dog with the dilemma of having to concentrate on both you and the approaching dog at the same time.

4   **Strangers' (pants-) legs are taboo:** Dogs are only trying to be nice when they give everyone they meet a friendly greeting, but it's usually not appreciated. If your dog can't resist doing it, then training with a long line is in order. This is how it works: If you see your dog eyeing a stranger, pick up the long line (without looking at or speaking to your dog) and nonchalantly make a big detour around the object of his desire. When the dog follows, praise him enthu-siastically and reward him. Eventually, he'll get the idea that he should maintain a polite distance.

5   **With and without the leash:** A never-ending topic of discussion among many dog owners is whether an unleashed dog should be allowed to run up to a dog on a leash. He shouldn't, because it puts the leashed dog in a difficult position. After all, a dog on a leash can't get away and has trouble defending himself if things get out of hand. For this reason, many leashed dogs appear visibly stressed when they find themselves in a situation like this, as do their owners. So here, again, make a polite detour around both of them.

6   **Marking:** Male dogs mark enthusiastically and often (some females do, too). But piddling every-where without restraint is inappropriate, as well as unnecessary. You can teach your dog not to mark every park bench, planter, wall, and automobile tire he passes. And the obstacles on the agility course don't need to be watered, either.

7   **No "play hunting" of other animals:** Whether it's ducks and other birds, wild animals like rabbits and deer, or cats, every animal senses panic when it is being pursued. This is true even if your four-legged friend is just chasing after the animals for fun. That's why you have to restrain your dog right away, even as a puppy, if he starts chasing other animals like this.

Tricks for Four-legged Stars

What may seem like circus acts are really just clever tricks that owners can do with their dogs. Displaying perfect teamwork, dog and human skillfully perform amazing routines that they have rehearsed together without drills or pressure, relying instead on pleasure, praise, and rewards. And that's quite an achievement for both of them!

Some of the tricks look easy, like the "Twist" (❯ page 80), in which the dog learns to spin around at your signal. Others, however, seem difficult—for example, the "High Five," where the dog touches your hands with his paws (❯ page 69).

What's surprising is that talent is distributed just as randomly among our four-legged friends as it is with us humans. Whereas one dog can understand a complex exercise in no time and carry it out effortlessly, another has problems with even a seemingly simple task. That's why, here again, it's important to gauge the abilities of your four-legged teammate correctly, so that you can design a training program to suit the dog. And in case you still get a slightly uneasy feeling at the thought of circus acts, simply practice without an audience.

All the same, you mustn't forget the applause for your dog! After all, he has certainly earned it for his efforts.

High Five

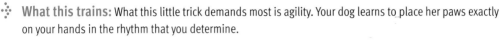

What this trains: What this little trick demands most is agility. Your dog learns to place her paws exactly on your hands in the rhythm that you determine.

What you need: A non-skid surface, so that the dog sits securely, and treats.

Many dogs learn the clapping game "High Five" very quickly, even if the exercise looks complicated at first. It's plain to see that most of them have fun practicing it—perhaps because the spectators get so excited when it works. The gesture originated in the United States, where it's common among athletes when they want to applaud a successful effort. If one teammate makes a fantastic play or scores a goal, another one holds the palm of his hand at about head height ("high"), and the successful player smacks it loudly with all five fingers of his hand ("five") in an expression of mutual congratulation. Outside of sports, two people often "High Five" each other when they want to show approval or complete agreement about something.

Goal of the game

"High Five," sometimes called "Gimme Five," exists in many variations. When we practice with the dog, we use the three-beat clapping rhythm that is customary among children. To do this, squat down in front of your dog. First, clap your hands together, then hold up one hand, palm facing the dog at her head height; the dog lifts the paw on that side and places it against your hand. Then clap again, hold up your other hand facing her, and the dog responds with her other paw. Finally, clap a third time and raise both hands toward the dog; she sits up on her hind legs, so she can place both front paws on your hands.

First one paw . . .

In the first step, teach the dog to lift her front paws as high as her head, for example, like this: Tell the dog to *sit;* holding a treat in your hand, move your hand above her nose until she eventually tries to reach it with a paw. If she touches your raised hand with her paw as she does this, reward her with the treat. Once the dog understands the movement, practice the same thing with the other paw. When it's working on both sides, practice without a treat in the clapping hand. If the dog places her paw against the palm of your hand, give her the treat from the other hand.

Practice on both sides until it goes smoothly. Don't practice the individual steps too often, though; instead, teach the sequence of movements slowly—two or three times per session are enough.

Two paws simultaneously

Now comes the more difficult part of this exercise: The dog has to place both paws against your raised hands, and she has to sit on her hind legs to do it. Once again, start with a food reward in the hand that you then move over her nose until she reaches for it with her paws—this time, however, she has to use both paws. If she does that, she gets the reward. If she only tries it with one paw, raise your hands a bit higher. Important: The dog must remain sitting when she does this. If she stands up on her hind legs, your hands were too high—keep trying until you find the right height. The bigger the dog, the

more trouble she'll have maintaining her balance. Be sure to take your time training her to sit up straight. Every time the dog gets a little higher, reward her—until your four-legged friend is actually sitting on her hind legs for the clap.

And now the three-beat rhythm

Once your dog has mastered all the individual movements, you can practice the complete exercise in a three-beat rhythm: clap hands, right hand to left paw; clap hands, left hand to right paw; and clap hands, both hands to both paws.

A verbal command is not essential for this exercise (you can, however, introduce one), because the hand clapping is such a powerful stimulus that the dog will be sure to respond to it and will quickly grasp what you expect of her. And now, have fun with this entertaining game!

1. Lift the paw: The owner teaches Monokel to lift her paw in order to reach his hand. In the beginning, she gets a reward as soon as she lifts her paw, but later on, only when she stretches a bit higher—until she finally reaches the palm of his hand.

2. Wrong side: Here everything is going smoothly and the paw is almost at the right height. However, Monokel is offering the wrong paw: When her owner lifts his right hand, Monokel should mirror him by lifting her left paw.

3. Left hand, right paw: This is correct. The owner holds the palm of his left hand up toward his Dalmatian at head height, and she places her right paw on it.

4. Now they've got it!: It's finally working on both sides. Monokel responds to her owner's raised hand with the correct paw.

5. Perfect: Monokel has understood the entire sequence of movements. She sits almost straight up on her hind legs to clap both of her owner's hands with her paws.

Roll Over

What this trains: When dogs feel good, they love to roll around on their back. With your help, this can be turned into a little coordination exercise.

What you need: Soft ground for the dog to roll on.

For this little trick, your dog has to have mastered the *down* command, because you start the exercise from this position. When the exercise is over, all it takes is a visual and verbal signal for the dog to do a sideward roll on the ground and finally land again on all fours.

Not on a full stomach

Only practice when the dog has completely digested his meal and hasn't just had a big drink from his water bowl. That's because the dog runs the risk of stomach rotation (gastric torsion) when his stomach is full of food or water.

Reliably on his side

First, put your dog in the *down* position. Squat down in front of him and, with a food reward in your hand, gradually get him to lie on his side. If he follows your hand for a bit, give him the treat. Practice this frequently, step by step, until your dog lies on the ground on his side. If it takes your dog several steps to get there, spread the exercise out over one or more days. In the next step, bring your hand with the food reward toward the dog's knee and then over his lower back. Now the dog has to twist around from the side position in order to reach the treat. In this stage, you can also introduce the verbal signal, for example, *Roll over!* Say it every time, just before the dog rolls from one side to the other.

On his legs

Once your dog has mastered the roll, reward the next step: Your dog should come out of the roll by standing on all fours. To do this, delay giving the treat after the roll until the dog stands up again without being asked. Gradually, you can start to stand up yourself for this exercise and merely indicate the roll with your hand. You can develop your visual signal from this, for example, a circular motion with your index finger. The clicker also works well with this little exercise (❯ page 40). For every improvement in the roll, give a click and a food reward.

1. Start with *"Down!"*: The owner and Pepe, a 15-month-old Border Terrier, are already an experienced team. "Roll Over" is part of their repertoire of games. For this exercise, the owner first puts his dog in the *down* position.

2. Tempting treat: The owner has a treat in his hand and uses it to entice his little Border Terrier out of the *down* position and over onto his side.

3. Roll over once: Pepe has understood the move. He willingly lies on his side. The owner brings the treat over Pepe's head to the other side, and in a flash the little dog rolls over nimbly along with it.

4. Perfect roll: Once Pepe has mastered rolling over, he doesn't get the treat until he stands up again.

Jump Through My Arms

What this trains: Your dog learns to perform a jump in close proximity to you. To do this, she must adjust her takeoff and height to match the position of your body. This is also a good fitness exercise.

What you need: Soft ground and treats.

If you have a dog who loves to jump and isn't too big, this trick is just the thing for both of you! Teach the exercise step by step so that, eventually, your dog jumps consistently and elegantly. First of all, the dog learns to jump over a human obstacle, namely, your arm. Start by squatting down and stretching your arm out to the side. Put your hand on a post, a tree, a fence, or something similar so that the dog can't veer to the side when she jumps. With a treat in the other hand, entice your dog to jump over your arm and praise her enthusiastically when she does it.

Closing the circle

Once that works smoothly, you can gradually move away from the side barrier and have the dog jump "free" over your outstretched arm. Practice that until the dog jumps over it reliably at your signal. Don't hold your arm too high yet, though, and stay in a squat. Gradually start using your other arm, holding it over the jump arm so that the dog barely notices this upper barrier. If this works well, you can keep closing the circle until the dog finally jumps through it with no difficulty. In this stage of the exercise, you can also introduce your verbal signal. Practice it patiently in small stages, but under no circumstance too often. Two or three rounds are enough, then it's time for a break. For every jump, reward the dog with lavish praise and a short game or treat.

Motivated to run along

Once your dog manages to jump through your arms reliably, gradually begin to stand up straight. Make sure that you first reinforce every newly achieved jump height before you go even a little higher. Adjust your final position very precisely to your dog's size and ability to jump. She should be able to make the jump easily. Some dogs can jump through a person's arms better if they get a bit of a running start. In order to motivate the dog to run toward you and jump, you can ask a second person to run with her, at first, and cheer the dog along.

1. A tree as a barrier: Jumping over an arm works best if you provide a barrier on one side, at first. Amy is enticed to jump with the other hand.

2. Free jump: Amy is no longer afraid of contact and now jumps "free"—which is to say without any side barrier—over her owner's arm.

3. Half circle: The owner starts using her other arm, too, but at first so that her female Irish Terrier barely notices it.

4. Full circle: It works even if the owner stands up. To do this, she forms a complete circle with her arms. The dog jumps through from back to front.

Jump on My Back

 What this trains: Your dog learns to coordinate his movements when jumping, so that he lands securely on your back and maintains his balance there.

What you need: Soft ground, a second person, treats, and possibly a clicker and target stick (❯ pages 40/64).

A little dog and a large child—the ideal team for this athletic exercise. Of course, grown-ups can play along, too. In this case, the training doesn't just keep your dog fit; it's also good exercise for you. Your dog will quickly learn how to do this trick if he doesn't have a basic problem with getting on your back.

It's best with two

Start by getting down on all fours with your dog sitting beside you. A second person should now get the dog to approach your back so that he eventually jumps up on it. To do this, your helper stands on your other side facing the dog and, treat in hand, lures him toward your back. You can also teach this exercise with a clicker and target stick. It works like this: Your helper touches your back with the target stick. As soon as the dog touches the stick, he gets a click. Gradually raise the stick until the dog puts his front paw on your back and finally jumps up. Now, you can also introduce the appropriate signal. To prevent the dog from just jumping over your back or hopping right back down again, your helper can stand close enough to your back to create a natural barrier for the dog.

Several verbal signals

For this exercise, introduce not just a verbal signal for jumping up (for example, *"Up!"*) but also one

 EXPERT TIP

Introduce the release signal

In your vocabulary list of signals used for training your dog, you definitely need a release signal. You use it to tell the dog that a particular exercise is over. If you don't have a signal, the dog will be forced to stop every exercise on his own, and at a moment that suits him. Give some thought to what you want to use as a release word, for example, *"All done!"* or *"Go on!"*

1. Ready to go: The owner gets down on all fours and has Pepe sit next to him. The owner's helper has a treat and a clicker in his hand. The owner gives Pepe the command to jump up. The helper clicks as soon as Pepe's paws touch his owner's back.

2. Successful jump: The little Border Terrier Pepe is always ready for a trick. He learned how to jump on his owner's back in no time.

3. Secure stance: Pepe has learned to balance his body so that he stands securely on his owner's back. He stays there until he gets the signal *"Off!"* Actually, this little trick is almost circus ready. Pepe and his owner will certainly get a big hand if they have an audience.

for jumping down (*"Off!"*). This way, you can teach the dog to remain standing on your back until you give him the command to jump down. With a lot of training, your dog will eventually be able to jump on your back even without a second person. Be patient practicing this little trick, for example, by having your helper move farther and farther away.

77

Go Backward

 What this trains: For this exercise, your dog has to pay close attention to you—even from a distance. To make it work, you have to maintain eye contact.

What you need: Treats as a reward, clicker (❯ page 40), and possibly a leash.

You can easily incorporate this demanding exercise into your daily walk.

A step back

Place your dog so that he stands facing you. Now walk calmly and slowly toward him until he takes a step backward—then, click and treat. Very important: So that the dog doesn't feel threatened by your approach, don't bend forward or walk toward him too briskly. Practice repeatedly two or three times in succession (spread out over a few days) until the dog clearly understands that you want him to move backward.

Step by step

Now comes the second step. To do this, walk toward your dog again in a calm, friendly manner without bending over him, but don't click until he takes a second step backward. This way you will gradually increase the number of steps until he consistently takes four or five steps backward. Then you can introduce verbal and visual signals, for example, *"Back up!"* while you put your arms behind your back. Now, try to send your dog backward (without walking along). Once again, have the dog stand facing you, but this time don't walk toward him; instead, just give the verbal and visual signals. Wait patiently. If your dog makes the slightest movement backward, click. This way you can gradually teach him to go backward even without your help. If the dog sits down as he goes backward, you can do one of two things: Wait patiently (without a signal) until he stands up on his own again, give him a click (and a treat) in return, and continue the exercise. Or, put his leash on (if he was off-leash), take two or three steps backward—the dog will follow—and begin the exercise again at this new position. Important for the timing: Click as he moves backward and not once he has stopped, otherwise, he could mistake the click as reinforcement for stopping. Once the dog has reliably mastered taking three steps backward and you want to train him to take another step, remember to click as he makes the fourth step.

1. Eye contact: Pluto's owner called him over to her and made eye contact with her Turkish Shepherd mix. Now it's time to concentrate: Pluto has to take a step backward.

2. Stay calm and stand up straight: The owner takes one step toward her dog, slowly and standing up straight—Pluto backs up a step. Important: As soon as the dog shows signs of stress, stop the exercise (check your own technique—maybe your dog feels threatened by you). After a brief pause, start again calmly.

3. Walking backward: Pluto already knows the signal. His owner says *"Back up!"* and puts her arms behind her back. The dog walks straight back very nicely. The owner has paid attention to that from the beginning.

4. Eight steps backward: The owner remains standing and gives her dog only the verbal and visual signals: Pluto obediently takes seven to eight steps backward without a problem. The pair has been practicing this trick for weeks.

Twist

 What this trains: Attentiveness and coordination are required here, because the dog has to turn once around her own axis without jumping or swerving to the side.

What you need: Possibly a clicker and a target stick (❯ pages 40/64) and treats.

The Twist is also an element in Canine Freestyle (❯ pages 140/141). To do it, the dog spins once around her own axis. In the beginning, she gets a treat for every small movement in the correct direction, but eventually only for the entire twist. You can also use the target stick to lead the dog around by the nose (❯ page 64). It works like this: The dog always gets a click when she follows the target stick with her nose and touches it.

The goal is to twist her body

First, have the dog stand as close as possible beside or in front of you so that you can reach her muzzle with your hand. Take a treat in your hand. Hold it in front of her nose a little below her muzzle and slowly move your hand away from you in an arc. Reward the dog when she follows the circular movement of your hand for a short distance by bending her body. That sounds simple, but it has to be learned. At first, the dog may back up a few steps in order to reach the hand with the treat, or she may stretch her neck and jump for your hand.

Practice in small steps

Practice the circling motion in small steps. To do this, lead your dog back into the starting position. Hold the treat hand below her nose and move your hand only a short distance to the side. If she now moves her entire body forward, praise her and reward her.

If you practice the circle in very small steps like this, the dog will usually get the hang of the twisting motion very quickly. Now, you can also introduce the verbal signal for it, for example, *"Twist!"* Once the dog follows your treat hand with a neat turn, start rewarding her only after she turns around completely and arrives back in the starting position. After that, stop holding treats in the leading hand; instead, reward her from the other hand. Once that works reliably, raise your hand gradually higher. Eventually, your verbal signal and a small circling hand motion will be all it takes for the dog to execute a twist.

1. Follow the treat: Amy the Beauceron is an experienced trick dog. Her owner holds a treat in her right hand and uses it to lead the dog in a circle.

2. Reward in stages: In the beginning, every little turn in the right direction earns praise and a reward.

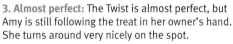

3. Almost perfect: The Twist is almost perfect, but Amy is still following the treat in her owner's hand. She turns around very nicely on the spot.

4. Amy does the Twist: Eventually, the owner only has to make a circling motion with her hand and give the appropriate verbal signal for her Beauceron to do the Twist.

Jump Through My Legs

 What this trains: Coordination and attentiveness are required for the dog to jump through his owner's legs with the correct timing.

What you need: Soft ground, treats (or a toy), and possibly a target stick and clicker (❯ pages 40/64).

For small dogs, this trick is no big deal. Most learn it in a flash. This exercise is also suitable for a child and a dog if both have already learned how to train together.

Just run through the first time

Start by getting rid of any fear of contact that the dog may have. To do this, stand with your legs apart; the dog sits or stands behind you. Now, entice him to walk under your legs with a treat (or a toy) and praise him enthusiastically if he follows the treat or toy in your hand. Here's how it's done with the target stick: Stand with your legs apart and have the dog stand behind you. Hold the stick first between and

then in front of your legs. Each time the dog's muzzle touches the stick, he gets a click and a treat. Depending on how cautiously your dog walks between your legs, gradually bring your legs together so that the passageway keeps getting narrower. The goal is for the dog to cooperate without showing any fear of contact.

Once that works, bend your knee and rest one foot against the other to form a triangle. Lure the dog through it. In the beginning, it is enough if the dog climbs over the hurdle (your foot). Consistently going through your legs and stepping over the foot-hurdle are two steps that you should teach in succession. Once that goes smoothly, you can motivate the dog to jump over the foot-hurdle. To do this, encourage him with a friendly tone of voice and hold the hand with the lure (or the target stick) a bit higher. Practice the jump just two or three times. Once the jump works well, introduce the signal—and do it just before the dog jumps.

Soft landing

Once your dog can perform the jump effortlessly, you can move your foot a little higher. Or you can stand a little farther away from your dog and then have him take a running start before jumping through your legs (increase the distance very gradually!). Make sure that your dog is relaxed when jumping so that he lands softly.

1. The first time through: The owner starts by standing with her legs spread apart. She uses a treat to lure Bobby, her two-year-old Prague Ratter, through her legs until he can do it effortlessly and with no fear of contact.

2. Little jump: In the second training session, the owner bends her knee and rests her foot against the other leg. Now the task is a bit harder for Bobby. The little dog follows the treat hand without hesitation.

3. Big jump: The owner stands up straight, one leg bent. At her signal, her dog Bobby jumps through her legs. In return, he gets enthusiastic praise and a treat to keep him motivated.

Put Away the **Toy**

 What this trains: Sharp wits and the ability to work independently are needed here: The dog combines two separate actions to create a sequence.

What you need: A toy; a basket, bucket, box, or bowl; treats; and a clicker.

A place for everything and everything in its place: Let your dog put away his own toys!

Toy and toy box

First, teach your dog to pick up a toy and carry it around in his mouth for a while. This is a good clicker exercise (❯ page 40). Place a toy near the dog and click when he puts his nose near it (don't forget the treat). Once he understands that you're interested in the toy, the next step is to click every time he picks up the toy until you're sure that he understands that, too. Then, don't click again until your dog holds the toy in his mouth for a while. Timing

is important here: You have to click while the dog is holding the toy and not just after he drops it. Otherwise, he'll think his task is to let go of it. In the second lesson, teach the dog to look in the container that you have provided for this game. First, put the toy away again. Click as soon as the dog approaches the container (but don't give him any verbal or visual signals to do this). Once he understands that the container is important here, don't click again until he touches the container with his nose. Once that goes smoothly, the dog has to look into the container—click and reward him when he does it.

Combine the actions

Once the dog performs both actions reliably—picking up the toy and looking in the container—practice combining them: He has to put the toy in the container. To do this, place both objects in front of your dog. If he picks up the toy and turns his head toward the container or even takes a few steps toward it, click. Repeat that—over several training sessions—until the dog understands that he should take the toy to the container. The next clicks come in stages: when he approaches the container with the toy in his mouth, when he is very close, when he eventually looks into the container, and, finally, when he drops the toy into the container. Once the dog is carrying out the entire sequence reliably, introduce the signal just before he picks up the toy.

1. Carry the toy: First Pepe, a 15-month-old Border Terrier, learns to pick up his toy and carry it for a while. His owner reinforces every little success with a click.

2. Look in the basket: In the second lesson, the owner teaches Pepe to look in the little basket. To do this, he clicks at first every time Pepe approaches the basket, then only when Pepe touches the basket with his nose, and finally not until he looks inside.

Pepe gets the idea: Now Pepe has to learn to go toward the basket with the toy in his mouth. At first, the dog gets a click he just looks toward the basket with the toy. Now, Pepe understands that he is supposed to go to the basket.

Everything's tidy: At the signal *"Tidy up!,"* Pepe picks up his toy, runs with it to the basket, and drops it in. This also works without the clicker now, because the dog has made the connection between the sequence of actions and the signal. You can take several days to teach this exercise—depending on how quickly your dog understands what's expected of him.

85

Caps Off

 What this trains: In this entertaining trick, coordination and the ability to work independently are important. Teamwork like this strengthens the bond between you and your dog.

What you need: A cap (with a bill), treats, and a clicker (❯ page 40).

This act really is circus material: At your signal, your dog pulls the cap from your head. It's ideal on a hot day, and always a crowd pleaser. The training for this is not difficult. It's a good clicker exercise (❯ page 40).

Get the cap

First, the dog has to learn to take hold of the bill of the cap with his mouth. To do this, squat down and place the cap on the ground in front of him. You don't need to give him a signal; simply wait until he sniffs at the cap inquisitively. Reward him with a click and a treat. Repeat this a few times and then

take a break before you run through the whole thing again (possibly not until the next day).

Pick up the cap

Once the dog understands that the cap is what's important here, practice the next step with him. Now, he has to pick up the cap in his mouth, so instead of clicking whenever the dog touches the cap with his nose, you have to wait patiently. This way, the dog realizes that simply sniffing at the cap is no longer enough and will take more drastic action. As soon as he picks up the cap in his mouth, click—until he understands that, too.

Pull the cap from your head

Now, for the high point: Put the cap on your head, but loosely enough at first so that it can be pulled off easily. Now, bend down a bit toward the dog until he gets the idea of sniffing at the cap—then, click and reward. Now build up the action step by step until the dog pulls the cap from your head.

If you use the clicker, this can happen very quickly. Once the dog performs a step reliably—for example, he takes the cap in his mouth—don't click for it again. Instead, wait patiently until he pulls harder on the cap—then, click each time until that goes smoothly. Once the dog is performing the exercise reliably, introduce the verbal command.

1. Touch the cap: Toni and his owner have been practicing this trick for a week. In the beginning, the owner always clicked when Toni touched the cap with his nose.

2. Pick up the cap: Now the owner no longer clicks when her little mixed-breed dog touches the cap, but instead waits patiently until he picks up the cap by the bill. She practices it with him several times until Toni does it consistently.

. Pull off the cap: The owner tilts her ead toward Toni in order to get him to ouch the cap. That works well. Toni akes the bill in his mouth right away nd gets a click and a treat in return.

. Trick perfected: As soon as Toni nderstands what he has to do, his wner introduces the command *"Caps ff!"* Neither dog nor owner minds that is trick is hard on her hairdo.

The Perfect Bow

What this trains: The dog practices coordination and attentiveness in this exercise, which requires him to take a bow and remain in this position until you give the release signal.

What you need: Treats and possibly a clicker (❯ page 40) or a target stick (❯ page 64).

The bow is part of the behavioral repertoire of every dog, whether large or small. It results from the typical invitation to play. When you want to elicit this behavior deliberately, you have to train it step by step.

First step

Start by having the dog stand in front of you. In the first step, the dog has to put his head down on the floor. Get him to do this by luring him with a food reward. Give your dog the treat when he follows your hand to the floor with his nose—and praise him enthusiastically, as well.

Second step

So that the dog actually makes a play bow in this second step, don't be satisfied when he puts his head down. Start by luring him down again with the treat hand, but don't give him the food reward; instead, carefully slide your hand under his nose toward his front paws. Now, to reach the treat, the dog has to lower himself onto his front legs—in return, he gets enthusiastic praise and, of course, the treat. Your dog may go from this position directly into the *down* position. Then, your timing is important: Praise your dog at the precise moment he rests on his elbows, so that he associates the reward with this position.

Once he has understood, you can introduce the appropriate signal for it, for example, *"Take a bow!"* Important: End the bow with your usual release word again (❯ Expert Tip, page 76). The release word must come quickly, especially in the beginning, so that the dog doesn't go into the *down* position.

If you have already conditioned your dog to a target stick (❯ page 64), you can use it to practice this trick. Here, the dog follows the target stick instead of your treat hand. Click each time the dog touches the stick in the correct position. Don't forget the reward! Another option: Click whenever the dog happens to stretch, and build up this behavior into a bow.

1. **Stand still:** Pluto, the owner's big Kangal mix, demonstrates here how he learned the bow. The dog begins this exercise in the standing position.

2. **Nose to the ground:** The owner has a treat in her right hand—reason enough for Pluto to follow her hand down to the ground with his nose. In the beginning, he gets a treat for this.

3. **Front legs on the ground:** Now, Pluto also has to put his elbows on the ground. For this step, his owner slides her hand under his nose toward his front paws. Pluto can only reach her hand if he lowers the front half of his body. At precisely this moment, his owner rewards him.

4. **Bow:** Eventually the visual signal is all it takes— the owner swings her right arm downward and bends over slightly.

Thinking Games to Stay Mentally Fit

When you spend time regularly with your four-legged friend, you do more than just strengthen his trust in you and reinforce the bond you share—you also teach the dog how to learn. This yields wonderfully long-lasting results, because, with time, the process becomes more dynamic. It's rather like foreign-language learning with us: The more foreign languages we know, the easier it is for us to learn another one. But back to our four-legged friends: The more you teach your dog—always provided it's done without pressure and involves lots of praise and pleasure—the more easily he handles new and more challenging tasks. Humans and animals are similar in yet another respect: Thinking is hard work. That's why even the games on the following pages, which all emphasize reasoning ability, are very tiring for your dog. Don't forget that, and make sure you take a break after every tricky task—for instance, by playing a little game of tug-of-war (❯ Praising and rewarding correctly, page 46) or letting him romp around to his heart's content with his favorite toy. In any case, your clever dog has certainly earned it! Never lose your patience if your dog can't solve these puzzles right away. With dogs—just as with us—intelligence is expressed in different ways.

Shell Game

What this trains: In familiar surroundings, the dog learns to concentrate fully on your actions, interpret them correctly, and find the treat under the right cup.

What you need: At least two colored cups and treats.

In this game, you can really watch how your dog thinks! As you might expect, it is tiring for the dog. That's why familiar, quiet surroundings are especially important. Approach this game calmly and patiently, and teach it step by step. The dog's task is to find the treat under the correct cup—even if you switch the cups.

Where's the treat?

In the first step, show the dog what this game is all about. The dog sits in front of you and watches as you place a treat under a cup. Then, tell your dog to get the treat. Depending on her temperament, she may tip over a cup with her nose or just sniff at it. Praise her enthusiastically and let her eat the treat. Once the dog has it figured out—treat under cup— add a second cup to the game.

Playing with two cups

Place the two cups slightly apart on the floor. Now put a treat under one cup as the dog watches from the *sit* position. Lift up both cups, one after the other, in order to show the dog that there's a treat under one, but nothing under the other. Go about it quietly and calmly so that the dog can concentrate on what you're doing. As before, tell the dog to get the treat.

If she goes to the correct cup (or tips it over), praise her lavishly and give her a reward. If she picks the wrong cup, wait patiently until she turns to the right one—then, praise her and reward her.

Only when the dog goes consistently to the correct cup every time can you move on to the next step in this concentration exercise.

Switch the cups

Now, it really gets exciting. Once again, set up two cups in front of your dog and let her watch as you place the treat under one. But now switch the cups, sliding each one into the spot previously occupied by the other.

Do this very calmly and slowly so that the dog has no trouble following your movements. Now, tell her to get the treat. Does she go directly to the

correct cup? Congratulate her for this bull's eye! Praise her lavishly and stop for today—such a successful beginning is enough for now. It's more likely, however, that the dog will head for the wrong cup because that's where you put the treat first. In that case, wait patiently until she turns to the correct cup. Praise her for this and, of course, give her the food reward.

Try it once again calmly and watch your dog as you do it: How long can she follow you with her gaze while you switch the two cups?

In any case, two or three rounds of this game are plenty. Then, put all the cups away. Now it's time to unwind with a relaxing little game (❯ Praising and rewarding correctly, page 46)!

Does it work with three cups?

Try to practice this game several times with your dog over the next few days. It's great to watch the dog's concentration gradually increasing until she finally manages to follow your actions to the end and comes to the correct conclusion: Aha, the treat is under this cup!

Once the game works well with two cups, you can even try it with a third. But be careful: Don't let your dog get frustrated with the Shell Game.

It is very important to teach this game slowly and very calmly. Obviously, there is no scolding during the Shell Game, only praise—and if something is too difficult for the dog, you can make it easier by going back to an earlier step (❯ Expert tip, page 31).

Variations for outdoors

Arrange the cups in a triangle with about 5 yards (5 m) between each pair. Position yourself and your dog in the middle of the triangle.

Start by placing a treat under each cup while the dog watches; then, let your dog look for them. The point here is that she understands there's something under the cups.

Now, things get more complicated. Once again, stand in the middle with your dog. Have the dog *sit*. Now, go from cup to cup and pretend to put a treat under two of them, but actually hide a food reward under just the third cup. Then, go back to your dog. Turn your upper body in the direction of the cup with the treat and look at it. The idea is that the dog learns to watch you closely, because your posture and gaze show her the correct direction.

Now, send the dog to look for the treat. If she doesn't head for the correct cup immediately, don't intervene. As soon as she reaches the correct cup, make a big fuss over her success. The dog rewards herself by overturning the cup and eating the treat. Cautious dogs may hesitate to knock over the cup, in which case you can help by going to the cup and giving your dog the treat hidden beneath it.

To keep the game exciting, hide the treat under a different cup for each new round. It gets even more difficult if you gradually increase the distance between cups. Then, the dog has to travel farther.

However, limit yourself to two or three rounds in a row. You need a lot of patience for this game. Some dogs require a bit more time than others.

1. Reward cup: Amy already understands what's going on in this game: There's a treat under one of the cups. Now her owner practices with her so that she sees which cup hides the reward.

2. Watch closely: Once again the owner shows Amy that there's a reward under one cup but not under the other. Then she tells the dog to get the treat.

Brainwork: Now it gets tricky. Once again, there's a treat under just one cup. Amy saw exactly which one. But then her owner switches the cups. Now, where's the treat?

Got it!: Amy needs a few tries in order to figure it out: The cup with the treat has moved! In the beginning, she couldn't follow the sliding motion to the end because it was difficult for her to concentrate so much. After two or three days, though, she manages to do it. Now, the dog makes a bee-line for the correct cup.

Follow My Gaze

What this trains: In this game, too, the emphasis is on your dog's ability to concentrate and, of course, to reason. She has to follow your gaze.

What you need: Treats.

Like the Shell Game, this mental exercise is exciting: How well can your dog follow your gaze? If you have been training together for a while, whether with games or sports, chances are pretty good that your dog will quickly grasp what's going on here. However, even if it doesn't work right off the bat, this exercise is wonderful for communicating with the dog through eye contact.

All it takes is a glance

In the beginning, you should try out the game someplace that is familiar to your dog and where she feels secure, so that she is not distracted. Later,

you can also try practicing with more distractions, for example, outdoors.

Your dog should sit quietly in front of you. Squat down facing her so that you can easily stretch out both arms. Have a treat hidden in one hand. Now, extend your arms and turn your head to look very clearly in the direction of the hand with the treat. Tell your dog to get the treat by saying something like *"Get the treat!"* As you do this, watch your dog out of the corner of your eye. If she heads for the wrong hand first, ignore it and wait patiently. If she has a hard time following your gaze, it can be very helpful for her if several people in the room stare at the correct hand.

Patience is important here. Give your dog plenty of time to understand what you expect of her. Practice only two or three times with the minimum requirement that the dog merely glance in the correct direction. Later, you can expect a more definite reaction. Eventually, the dog should run to the correct hand and get the treat hidden there.

From one hand to the other

Once everything is going smoothly and your dog follows your gaze with no problem, raise your standards: Place yourself in front of the dog as described above, arms outstretched. Look directly at the hand with the treat. Then, switch the treat from one hand to the other behind your back and look in the opposite direction.

Give your dog the signal to get the treat. Will she understand the switch and interpret your gaze correctly? Once again, teach this step very gradually;

1. New assignment: The owner and his female Dalmatian Monokel regularly do obedience training. They make a great team, but this task is new for both of them. The owner holds a treat hidden in his left hand. Monokel has to sit and wait patiently.

2. Find the treat: Now, the owner turns his head to stare at the hand with the treat. He gives Monokel the command *"Find the treat!"* She has to follow his gaze and pick the correct hand.

praise and reward her initially for any sign of heading in the desired direction. Once your dog has learned to follow your gaze, she'll have a much easier time following directions in many other games. Even in "Find the Treat Bag" (❯ pages 38/39), she can get her bearings from you, provided your posture and gaze both point in the direction of the treat bag. This will make the "Go to. . . " game (❯ pages 100/101) an easy matter for the dog and will also provide welcome assistance in the "Shell Game" outdoors (❯ page 91).

3. Follow my gaze: This time the owner switched the treat to his other hand behind his back, and now he turns his head to look at this hand. Monokel understands right away and follows his gaze to the correct hand.

Find the Right One

····❖ **What this trains:** This game fosters the dog's ability to reason and to concentrate.

What you need: A few of the dog's toys (she should know their names) and possibly a clicker (❯ page 40).

This wonderful game can be played anytime and is lots of fun for all participants—as well as for spectators. After a little practice, your dog will prove to be an expert at understanding exactly what you want and bringing it to you.

Associate the toy with the name

To do this, your dog should know the names of some of her toys, for example, ball, rope, bone, rabbit, teddy bear, and so on. Practice that by placing a toy in front of her and saying its name just before she picks it up in her mouth. You can also use the clicker as reinforcement (❯ page 40). Later on, ask your dog to fetch a specific toy and click or praise her enthusiastically when she gives it to you. Natu-

rally, she gets a reward, too. If your dog is reluctant to pick up the object, it is enough if she just nudges it. Many dogs quickly learn to recognize some toys by name this way.

Make distinctions

But can your dog also distinguish one toy from another? Try it out: Take two toys that you are sure your dog knows by name and place them a short distance from your dog. Now, tell her to bring a specific toy to your, for example, *"Bring the ball!"* If she runs to the ball right away and brings it back, this was either beginner's luck or you have a four-legged genius—leave it at this initial success!

If it doesn't work right away and your dog brings the wrong toy, stay upbeat, but don't say anything; instead, put the toy back with the other one. Now, ask your dog once again to bring the ball. As soon as she runs to the ball and brings it back to you, praise her or click and make a big fuss over her. Of course, she also gets a reward.

Don't get too ambitious, though: One success is enough in the beginning. Practice this game no more than two to four times per session. With time, you can gradually increase the number of toys. If you notice that it's getting to be too much for the dog, go back to a simpler version of the game and reinforce this before you try the next step (❯ Expert tip, page 31).

1. Setting up for the game: Flocke, the little female mixed breed, waits patiently while her owner arranges "Mole" and "Bone" next to each other.

2. That's right: The owner tells Flocke to bring "Mole." The dog does it correctly, without hesitation.

3. Flocke knows what's what: Flocke heads straight for "Mole," picks it up, and carries it back to her owner. The dog gets a reward each time she does this, which keeps her in the mood to play. Flocke usually has no problem distinguishing among three toys, either (❭ photo, page 96).

A Game **for Puzzle-Lovers**

 What this trains: In this game, the dog has to be observant and reason correctly. This requires concentration and patience—and sometimes dexterity, too, as in this case.

What you need: A wooden puzzle toy—many different models are available online and in some pet stores, or you can design and build one yourself.

For the dog to enjoy this game, you have to let her take her time, so that she can arrive at a solution—and, of course, a tasty treat will spur her on.

First let her sniff
Puzzle toys for dogs come in many different varieties. Here's how this one works: A treat is dropped into the opening of a rotating cylinder, which can be turned using the round knobs. Sooner or later, the treat will fall into the drawer below. By tugging on the rope, the dog finally pulls out the drawer with the treat.

Some dogs are frightened of new things. They should have an opportunity to convince themselves that it is perfectly harmless. To do this, place the toy on the floor and let the dog simply sniff it, at first. Then put your dog in the *sit* or *down* position and let her watch as you put a tasty treat into the opening. Now, tell her to get the treat. Give the dog plenty of time to work on her task. Don't keep talking to her while she's busy with it—let her take her time mulling it over. As soon as the dog figures out on her own what to do—for example, push one of the knobs slightly (or just sniff at it)—praise her lavishly for this achievement. She has earned a reward for even the smallest attempt. The next time, wait a bit longer until she does a little more—then, give her the reward!

Thinking is hard work
If you have the feeling that your dog is baffled, show her how it works without saying a word. Every time she plays the game, let her eat the treat from the drawer. Don't practice more than two or three times—regardless of how successful the dog was. If the dog gets impatient the first few times and tries frantically to get the treat, pick it up and have her *sit* again. If the next attempt doesn't go any better, call off the game.

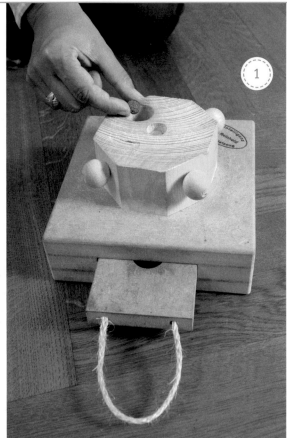

1. Drop in the treat: This is the owner's job. The dog should watch her do it, so that she knows: There's a yummy reward for me in this strange thing.

2. The right turn: Flocke loves puzzles, so she tries hard even for a perfectly normal treat. Her owner lets the dog take her time investigating, and keeps a good grip on the toy, so that it doesn't slide away. Flocke pushes on the knob until she hears something drop.

3. Now pull: Flocke is familiar with the game and knows: Once I hear this sound, the treat is mine. She uses her paw to pull out the drawer, then enjoys the reward for her patience and reasoning skills.

Go to ...

 What this trains: In this game, too, the dog has to reason and concentrate in order to assign a name to the correct person.

What you need: At least two or three family members or friends whose names your dog knows.

This is a nice party game for humans and dog alike. Even young children can take part if an adult is present.

Who's who?

The prerequisite here is that the dog knows the players by name, for example, members of the family. Dogs usually learn the names of their people without any effort. Give it a try—you'll be amazed! If it doesn't work reliably with everyone yet, stand opposite someone whose name the dog should know. Give your dog the signal *"Go to Nina!"* or *"Go to John,"* depending on the person's name. Now Nina or John lures the dog over with a treat and

makes a big fuss over the dog when she comes to them. This is also a good clicker exercise, especially if the dog has trouble keeping the names straight (❯ page 40). In the beginning, click every time the dog takes a step toward the named person. Gradually ask more of the dog by waiting for a second or third step before you click, until the dog finally reaches the goal.

Small circle for beginners

Once the dog knows all the participants by name, the game can begin. The players sit in a fairly large circle around the dog and have a few treats ready. Your dog sits in the middle and waits for the first signal: *"Go to. . . !"* If she makes the right choice and heads for the named person, she gets an enthusiastic welcome and a treat. Important—and not always easy for young children: Do not lure the dog with the treat. It's best if you hide the treat hand in your lap or behind your back. If the dog runs to the wrong person first, that person simply doesn't react or even look at the dog. Give the dog enough time to decide what to do. Once she finally goes to the correct person, she gets a big hello and the reward. If the game is new for your dog, you should make the radius of the circle fairly small, because this way your dog always arrives at the right address quickly. If she makes a mistake, she only has to take a step or two and she's at the right person.

The more reliably she has mastered the game, the larger the circle can be.

1. Entertaining game: Alex, a female Golden Retriever, sits patiently in the middle of the circle and waits to find out what she'll have to do in this game.

2. "Go to Timmi!": Three-year-old Timmi wonders if Alex knows his name. It works! The dog heads straight for the child, and he can give her a reward.

3. New goal: Now it's the child's turn to give the dog a signal. He sends Alex to the handler.

For advanced students

Tests have shown that dogs are even capable of reasoning by process of elimination. Try it yourself: Have a stranger sit down in a circle of people that your dog knows by name. Now, the dog has to head straight for this person. Give her the command *"Go to . . . (name of the unfamiliar player)!"* What does the dog do? Give her plenty of time, and don't irritate her with too many commands. If she doesn't immediately figure out which person you mean, she will quickly learn by trial and error.

Pull It Out

 What this trains: Agility, concentration, and reasoning ability are what your four-legged friend needs for this game.

What you need: A treat bag with treats, a fairly strong piece of twine, and a low table, dresser, cabinet, or something similar as a hiding place.

This game is a lot of fun and can be played at any time. Your dog is allowed to look for her treat bag, but it is cleverly hidden. How does the dog get to it?

Prepare the treat bag

Tie a fairly strong piece of twine, about one yard (1 m) long, around the treat bag, which you already have filled with treats. Make a big knot at the end of the twine, so that the dog can take hold of it easily. Alternatively, you can use one of the dog's toys instead of the treat bag. Reward the dog by playing with her once she succeeds in pulling the toy out of its hiding place.

Caution: Never wrap anything around a food reward! An overeager dog could wolf down the twine along with the reward.

Start out simply

Once you have tied the twine to the treat bag or toy, push the object a short distance under a dresser, cabinet, or similar piece of furniture, but not too far. There shouldn't be enough room beneath the furniture for the dog to stick her nose under it because, after all, the point of the game is for the dog to pull the object out. During these preparations, your dog sits next to you and watches you. Now, tell her to bring her treat bag to you—and wait patiently. She'll probably look under the hiding place but won't be able to reach the bag. Now, it gets exciting: Will she think up a strategy on her own? Perhaps she'll use her paw and scratch at the twine. Because the treat bag (or the toy) is not hidden very far under the furniture, it probably will emerge right away, and your dog will quickly grasp what this game is all about. Great—she's got it! Praise her enthusiastically and give her a treat from the treat bag. If she seems perplexed, then you can help her by pulling on the twine yourself. The next time, you should simplify the game so that the dog succeeds quickly and understands the connection between the treat bag (or toy) and twine. Gradually, begin hiding the object further and further beneath the furniture so that less and less twine is visible.

1. First attempt: Alex isn't familiar with this game yet. She watches eagerly as her owner hides her beloved treat bag beneath the coffee table. Then she gets the signal to bring her treat bag. But how?

2. Go for it!: The five-year-old female Golden Retriever knows a lot of tricks and games. After thinking it over briefly, she grabs the twine by the knot.

Very clever!: Alex pulls on the twine carefully and watches as her treat bag slowly emerges from beneath the table.

Got it!: As soon as the treat bag emerges, the dog picks it up and brings it to her owner.

Well deserved: This little thinking game was worth the effort. The retriever can now take a yummy morsel from the treat bag.

Take Your Dog to Work

Boredom beneath the desk? Not if you follow a little fitness program. Dog and owner can work out together.

Recent studies show that four-legged colleagues improve morale at the workplace. The stress level drops, social interaction benefits from having a dog on the team, and the lunch break is spent outdoors in the fresh air—all arguments in favor of canine co-workers. Naturally, this assumes that your dog obeys a few basic rules.

Sports for two

Exercise lifts everyone's spirits—even your dog's. You can try this at the workplace, for example, with office gymnastics. Five minutes of stretching and muscle exercises for you can also be a few minutes of training for your dog. To do this, park the dog between your legs in the *stand* position while you do a couple of exercises and, at your signal, have him practice *sit*, *down*, and *stand* in succession (or whichever of them he already knows). This is a very good exercise for training attentiveness and discipline with your dog.

Relieves strain on the spine: Stand up straight, legs slightly apart. Clasp your hands and stretch your arms up over your head, the palms of your hands turned outward. Now slowly bend forward, keeping your back straight, until your hands almost touch the ground. You put the dog in the *sit* position before you started; now, tell him to jump through your arms. Slowly stand up straight again.

Everything in order

Surely you also have a few toys for your dog in your office. While you clean off your desk just before quitting time, your dog should also tidy up: Have him put his toys away in a drawer or box (❯ pages 84/85). The game "Go Around the Obstacle" (❯ page 53) is also an excellent exercise to do, now and then. The waste paper basket, for example, makes a fine obstacle.

A treat ball or a fabric cube (❯ pages 24/25) that can be filled with dry food is ideal for the office. Or you can use a cardboard box and paper to create a food game (❯ pages 19/20). "Find the Treat Bag" (❯ pages 38/39) is just the thing for lunch breaks outdoors.

Play? Not now!

There's no question that, in the office, work comes first. Your dog has to respect this, too. If he finds it difficult and keeps trying to distract you with charming interruptions—a soft nose on your lap, a pleading stare that says *"Play with me!"*—then you'd better introduce definite rules for work time and dog time.

Use a clear visual signal that says to your dog: Now it's time to be quiet! To do this, take a towel, a scarf, or something similar and shake it vigorously so that the dog notices it. Then, hang it up somewhere, for instance, over the door. It must be clearly visible to the dog. Now, you have to be firm: If the dog comes over to you and wants your attention, ignore him. That means don't look at him, don't talk to him, don't touch him. Keep this up until you remove the towel from the door and shake it vigorously again. Then give the dog your attention, do a few minutes of office gymnastics for two, play a little game with him, or take a walk outdoors. Introduce the towel signal slowly: In the beginning, ten minutes is enough; then, gradually increase the quiet time. However, you should not expect your dog to wait patiently for more than four hours at a time.

Firms the thighs: Stand up straight, legs apart, arms stretched out horizontally. Bend forward at the hips. Slowly shift your weight from the right to the left leg, bending the weight-bearing leg. Stand up straight again, then shift your weight to the other side. Your dog is parked between your legs and at your signal does *sit*, *down*, *stand*. Repeat this exercise eight to ten times.

Strengthens the leg muscles: Stand with your back against the wall, legs apart. Slowly slide down until your upper legs and knees form a 90-degree angle. Keep your head up. With a treat in your hand, lure your dog through your legs in a weave.

105

DOG SPORTS FOR FOUR-LEGGED ATHLETES

Sports are good for you because they give you a
well-trained, healthy, trim body. This is just as true
for four-legged athletes as it is for those on two
legs. Staying fit while having fun together is the
theme of this chapter. Take the challenge!
You and your dog can become an
athletic dream team.

An Athletic Team: Dog and Human

From working dog to playmate: As our constant companion, the dog naturally accompanied us as we made the transition to a leisure society. Despite job stress and multimedia networking, people throughout the world have more time than ever before, both in hours of the day as well as in years of life. Many of us use this time for outdoor games and sports. This is ideal for our four-legged companions, because outdoor activities are among their favorite things. There's a lot to be said for just taking the dog along when you go bicycling, jogging, Nordic walking, hiking, swimming, or horseback riding. But sometimes that's easier said than done, because it's important to match your own condition, agility, and safety with the available opportunities as well as the abilities and fitness of your four-legged partner. Introduce your dog slowly and carefully to his particular role, and build up his stamina gradually, so that nothing spoils your enjoyment of this shared activity. Above all, though, if you participate in recreational sports with your dog, you must be able to control him, even without a leash and collar or harness; otherwise, fun and games can quickly turn dangerous. That's why it's important to train your four-legged friend thoroughly in good manners for leisure sports companions; it's a question of fairness for all involved.

Jogging and **Nordic Walking** Improve Condition

What this trains: For an adult dog who enjoys walking along with you, this is an ideal exercise and conditioning program.

What you need: Leash, harness, possibly a jogging belt, and drinking water for longer distances.

A run through the woods with your dog is a glorious thing, especially if your dog enjoys activity, because running is in his genes. His ancestor, the wolf, is adapted for running and can easily travel 20 to 30 miles (30 to 50 km) in 24 hours at an easy trot.

If you would like to take your dog jogging or Nordic walking, there are a few basics that you have to keep in mind: first of all, the age of the dog; then his condition; and, finally, how well he obeys. And there's another important point: Some dogs really don't enjoy running, just as some dislike bicycling. This is especially true of breeds or mixes that are not well suited physically for long-distance running, for instance, short-legged, heavy dogs like Basset Hounds, flat-faced breeds, and so on. But, occasionally, some perfectly athletic dogs are reluctant to trot along when their owner is jogging energetically over hill and dale. In that case, it makes no sense to insist on this athletic togetherness. Fortunately, there are plenty of alternatives!

Improve condition slowly

In order to find out if your dog is a happy jogger or walker, embark on a gradual training program for him. After all, it might just be your excessive demands that are spoiling your dog's enjoyment of jogging or Nordic walking.

Start with an easy training program once the dog is fully grown. That means about ten months for small dogs, one year for medium-sized dogs, and one and a half to two years for large and very large dogs. To be on the safe side, it's best to check with your veterinarian.

In the beginning, include short periods of running in your walks; three to five minutes are enough initially. When you do this, keep the dog on a loose leash; he should definitely know the *heel* command (❯ Practical tip, page 110). If the dog gets excited and tries to jump up on you, slow down until he runs along quietly for a few paces. Naturally, you should reward him with lavish praise and a treat.

Loping along

Regular walks with occasional periods of jogging are an ideal way to get your dog used to running along steadily with you. If that's going well after a few weeks and the dog is running along happily— with no sign of exhaustion—gradually reverse the ratio of running to walking. Be careful not to increase it too quickly, though: Running at your side for ten minutes is quite a challenge for your dog. Be sure to adjust your tempo to suit your dog: He should be able to run along at an easy lope.

Especially fit dogs can run with you for up to an hour, but make sure you take breaks along the way. You also should try to avoid asphalt surfaces for jogging or Nordic walking, in order to prevent the pads of your dog's feet from developing blisters.

In summer, the danger of overheating or even heatstroke is a serious problem for dogs (❯ Practical tip, "Why dogs pant" page 115); that's why it's better to train only in the morning and evening hours when temperatures are high. On the other hand, if the weather is hot and humid, you should just skip the training session. If you like to jog or walk very long distances with your dog, why not start a club of like-minded enthusiasts!

Motivate with breaks for play

In any case, you'll increase the fun-factor if you occasionally pause for a game during your run. Games like "Go Around the Obstacle" (❯ page 53), "Mountain Climbing Made Easy" (❯ pages 60/61), or "Tree Touch" (❯ pages 64/65) are especially suitable. This way, you can keep your four-legged partner in the mood to run by providing him with diversions and rewards.

❯❯ PRACTICAL TIP

Safety for your dog

When you are out in public with your dog, he should be able to walk beside you at your signal. You could, for example, use the command *"Heel!"* Your dog should walk calmly next to you, his shoulder near your knee, and always move at your pace. When your dog is about five to six months old, you can begin training this. Always practice in short training sessions (two to three minutes). Start with your leashed dog on your right side by your knee. The leash should hang loosely, but should not allow your dog too much freedom. Hold a few treats in your left hand, then begin walking at a normal pace. As soon as the dog leaves his position by your knee, you can use one of the following options to correct him: Stop walking, but don't look at him or speak to him; instead, wait patiently—if he returns to his position at your side, praise him enthusiastically and reward him with the treat from your left hand. If this correction doesn't work, try a different one: As soon as your dog runs ahead or lags behind, turn to the left; the leashed dog has to follow automatically. Once he is back in the correct position, give him lots of praise and a treat. When you finish practicing, don't forget to release the *heel* signal, perhaps by saying *"go on!"* or *"all done!"* In the beginning, have him *heel* for a just few yards, then slowly increase the distance. In three to four weeks, your dog should be able to carry out the command reliably.

1. With the leash: The owner jogs for short distances with her mixed-breed dog Toni. Occasionally, she walks for a few minutes or pauses for a brief game. A jogging belt is ideal.

2. Without the leash: Toni knows the *heel* command and goes along at an easy trot next to his owner. She releases the command again in a suitable area; then, Toni can run along at a greater distance from her.

3. Nordic walking: If you take your dog along when you go Nordic walking, you have to be able to rely on him, because this has to be done without a leash. The walking pace is ideal for this little mixed-breed dog, because the most it requires of him is an easy trot.

111

Bicycling with Your Dog at Your Side

···⫶ **What this trains:** Running along beside your bicycle is a great way for your dog to develop his muscles and improve his condition, provided you don't demand too much of him. In addition, the dog will be more willing to follow you because you're moving faster when you cycle.

What you need: Harness (no collar!), leash, water bottle, and possibly a rigid bicycle dog leash. For longer trips, perhaps a bicycle trailer or basket for your dog and energy bars (for the dog!).

Bicycling is just plain fun, especially when your dog runs along with you! Besides, it's an ideal fitness program for both of you, provided you go about it the right way. With a well-balanced training program and the proper equipment, even cycling trips are a possibility—you don't have to give them up just because you're a dog owner.

Tip: If you have a young dog, wait until he is fully grown before you let him run along when you go biking. That's because the constant stress affects his bones, and they won't be strong enough to take much athletic activity until he finishes growing.

Small breeds are fully grown at about ten months, medium-sized breeds at a year, large breeds—above 24 inches (60 cm) tall—keep growing until they are a year and a half old, and giant breeds like the Great Dane can even take up to two years. It's best to ask your veterinarian when you can start biking with your dog.

Fear of bicycles

Every four-legged novice cyclist should be introduced slowly and carefully to this strange contraption—because that's what the bicycle is for most dogs. Even dogs that run along well next to a bike are sometimes frightened if it gets to close to them. In sticky situations, this can be downright dangerous.

Dogs find the bicycle frightening for various reasons: They can't figure it out because it is rigid and shows no natural body language, so there's nothing for the dog to interpret. For example, it does not appease when it comes directly toward the dog. It also makes strange noises that baffle the dog. That's why you should familiarize your dog with the bicycle slowly, so that it doesn't get too close to him at first. This works well if you ask someone to take your dog on the leash while you push the bicycle. Because the dog should always stay to the right of the bicycle in traffic (next to the curb), position him on the right side of the bicycle even during the cycling warm-up. Let him walk along at a distance that seems comfortable for him.

Biking safely: A rigid bicycle dog leash that is attached to the frame of the bike lets you have both hands free for the handlebars and brakes. The dog runs alongside at a safe distance. This way, any sudden stops your dog makes are cushioned.

His tail, ears, and posture should all be relaxed. Your human helper holds the dog so that the dog's shoulder is even with your knee. A quiet conversation lets the dog know that you are not afraid of the inflexible contraption, so there's no reason for him to be worried. At first, it's enough if the three of you walk together for a short distance. Repeat this often until the dog accompanies you willingly at a reasonable distance. Only then can you mount the bicycle and ride along slowly while your helper continues to lead the dog on the leash, making sure that the dog doesn't get excited and start to run. As before, the dog should walk or trot along slowly at your knee. Alternately ride and push the bicycle until the dog has no trouble going along with these little changes in tempo. Now, it gets exciting: Take the leash in your hand (never wrap the leash around your wrist or the handlebar!) and start by having the dog walk along next to you for a short distance while you push the bike, and, then, while you slowly ride.

Safety measures

A rigid bicycle dog leash (dog jogger) that attaches to the frame of the bike is highly recommended. Pet stores carry a variety of models. This frees your hands for steering and braking, and any sudden stops the dog makes will be cushioned somewhat. You'll be safest cycling with your dog, though, if he knows some basic obedience commands and a few rules of the road.

To do this, he should be able to walk on a loose leash and heel off-leash reliably at your signal; a suitable signal would be something like *"Heel!"*

Once he has mastered that, you lessen the danger of your dog overtaking you (and possibly running in front of the wheel) or lagging behind as you're cycling. If he still doesn't know the signal, practice it with him at first without the bicycle (❯ Practical tip, page 110). Next, practice it with the bicycle. To do this, start by pushing the bike and, then, suddenly stop as soon as your dog leaves the *heel* position. Don't continue until he returns to the desired position. Once that's working well, practice by cycling slowly until your dog runs alongside reliably at your signal. Later on, you can practice little changes in tempo. The goal is that he always matches your speed and automatically stops when you stop.

Improve condition slowly

In principle, the dog should be able to run along beside the bicycle at an easy lope. Before you start cycling, make sure that he has plenty of opportunity to take care of his business. Galloping along for short stretches now and then is only appropriate on soft ground and without a leash. In addition, the dog should have learned not to run in front of the wheel (❯ below). There's always a risk of overtaxing the dog when cycling. After all, he can't set the pace himself. At the beginning of the season, start a

training program for your dog. A few intervals of five minutes cycling, five minutes pushing (= time for him to sniff around) are just right for the first few weeks. Then, gradually increase the cycling time. Watch for signs of exhaustion: For example, the dog can't keep the pace, he doesn't sniff around busily during the breaks, he pants more, and in general he seems unmotivated. In that case, you have to decrease your demands and train more slowly.

Relaxed on long rides

How long you can ultimately cycle together with your dog depends on a variety of factors: age, training condition, terrain (less asphalt, more soft ground), and weather (hot, humid weather is always worse than dry heat). In the warm summer months, you should schedule your bike rides for the morning and evening hours. A really well-

Acclimation phase on foot: Many dogs are suspicious of the bicycle. Give your four-legged friend an opportunity to get used to this contraption. For example, you could have a helper walk along, as in this photo.

trained dog can trot along for up to two hours, albeit with breaks (in the shade) and lots of time running off-leash (only in safe areas, of course). Longer trips will be very relaxed if you take along a bicycle trailer made especially for dogs. Then, your four-legged friend can take a break occasionally, and even unsafe stretches like busy streets can be managed stress-free this way. Some dogs tire more quickly than others and, then, should ride buckled up in a bicycle basket. Always carry water on your trips; you should also bring along a light snack for your dog, in order to prevent hypoglycemia.

>> PRACTICAL TIP

Why dogs pant

A dog has very few sweat glands, most of them on the paws. They're of little importance in regulating body temperature. An overheated dog cools down primarily by panting: With his mouth open, the dog breathes in through his nose and out through his mouth. In the process, water evaporates from the mucous membranes. The dog has to make up for this water loss by increasing the amount he drinks. That's why it is important to bring along drinking water for your dog in the summer and during strenuous exercise.

2. You and me and the bicycle: Toni is no longer afraid of the bike because his owner seems to have everything under control. He walks along next to her on a loose leash, perfectly at ease. Now his owner can even try riding slowly.

3. Independence for little legs: Toni runs along by his owner's knee. He has learned not to overtake the front wheel. For long trips, his owner attaches a bicycle basket for Toni.

Hiking with Your Dog—A Wonderful Adventure

What this trains: Stamina and condition. Besides, some quiet, stress-free time together strengthens the bond between dog and owner.

What you need: Leash and harness, possibly a dog backpack (so you can carry your dog) and hiking packs (for your dog to carry), paw protection if necessary (for hiking in the snow), and drinking water and a little food for the dog.

Most dogs are beside themselves with joy as soon as their owner gets out the hiking boots. They know what's coming: adventure and freedom.

Always keep to the path

However, it's only freedom for the dog if she can run along without a leash. You can find out from the city or local authorities where leash laws are in effect and where it's leashes off! To protect both environment and wildlife, the dog has to stay on the paths and should not be allowed to run back and forth, nosing around in the bush. It's the law (in some areas, it's even legal to shoot dogs that

chase or kill game or livestock). That's why an important prerequisite for a relaxed trip is a well-trained dog who comes immediately to your side when called.

Every dog can hike

Only fully grown dogs should accompany you on longer hikes, because the stress is bad for a young-ster's more pliable bones. Too much stress too soon can cause permanent damage. Your dog improves her condition just the way you do: by gradually increasing the length of the hiking route. On the day after a hike, take a break, because even dogs get aching muscles. Dogs that aren't crazy about running have problems with long hikes; moreover, too much jumping is bad for their joints. For hikes in the mountains, that's why you should choose fairly easy stretches and perhaps bring along a dog backpack to carry small dogs (available at the pet store).

My backpack, your backpack

If you aren't sure there's enough water along your route, take along drinking water for your dog. You should also bring some kibble or jerky as provisions for your hike. If you are planning on taking all-day hikes with your dog, you can teach her to carry her hiking gear herself: Hiking packs for dogs come in various sizes.

Give her plenty of time to get used to carrying them before you start your trip: first with empty packs for just a few minutes, then a bit longer, and,

1. Happy wanderers: Hiking with your dog is a glorious experience. Early in the season, start training together with short hikes to get in shape. With proper training, even longer routes will be no problem for your dog later on.

2. Doggy backpack: Pet stores carry special hiking packs in different sizes for dogs. This way, your four-legged friend can carry her provisions herself. Give her plenty of time to get used to it—before you start hiking.

gradually, with something inside. If your dog usually wears a harness, the packs will probably not bother her. In addition to a water bottle, water bowl (collapsible ones are available), and some provisions, you should have a small first-aid kit with bandages. For hiking in rough, mountainous terrain or on snow-covered trails, hiking boots for your dog are definitely in order—a dog can get sore feet from walking. However, this much equipment is usually only necessary for long hikes. Walking side by side through the countryside makes you happy to be alive—and tired. That's why you usually don't have to take a break for play when you're hiking; it just wears out your dog unnecessarily.

Water Sports with Your Dog

What this trains: A relaxed, safe program of aquatic training improves your dog's condition and stamina. For dogs with joint problems, exercise in the water is also very therapeutic.

What you need: Towel, water toy, a life vest for the dog, and drinking water (at the ocean).

Some breeds have an inborn love of the water. But dogs like Retrievers and Newfoundlands are not the only ones that like to swim. Once they get a taste of it, many dogs enjoy a refreshing dip in the river or lake. And if dog and owner discover they are both water rats, their passion can even develop into a heroic pursuit: Water rescue dogs working together closely with their handlers perform a great service. If you have this kind of ambition, you can develop your dog's ability to swim in a group that does water work or with a canine search and rescue unit (❯ page 150 and "Information" page 188).

Wet paws, warm praise

Nevertheless, every dog first needs to explore the water cautiously in order to find out just what kind of a strange element this is. Even a Newfoundland can turn out to be afraid of the water, at first. How much fun a dog has with water games depends first and foremost on acclimation and training.

You can even get puppies used to the water in a playful way by letting them take their time exploring the wet stuff along lake shores or river banks. If you seem fascinated and start playing in the water, your dog will certainly be curious and stick her nose in—she may even venture to dip in a paw. Then, praise her enthusiastically and let it go at that for the time being.

Getting acquainted slowly with this new, unfamiliar element is the best way for your dog to develop a love of the water.

For games of fetch later on, there are actual water toys for dogs in the pet store. When you throw the toy into the water, keep the distance short at first so that the dog can still feel the bottom beneath her paws. Once your dog seems completely at ease in the water, you can throw the toy so that she has to swim one or two strokes to get it. Back on land, she'll naturally expect a veritable hymn of praise for her masterful performance.

When you're getting the dog used to the water, compulsion in any form is taboo: A bad experience is the worst swimming teacher imaginable.

Retrieving is even more fun this way: A game in the water is a welcome change of pace for two-legged and four-legged players alike. Give it a try with your dog.

EXPERT TIP

If something happens . . .

In an emergency, it's good to know how to help your dog quickly if she's in danger. Dog owners should be familiar with first-aid measures for their pets, because accidents can happen anywhere, not just in the water. A course or a textbook will provide life-saving information on what to do in an emergency. If your dog stops breathing, you should know how to do cardiopulmonary massage. Important: Although your dog may seem perfectly fine again after a swimming accident, you should still take her to the veterinarian. Even a tiny amount of water in her lungs poses a serious health risk that often takes a few days to become apparent.

Born swimmers

All dogs have the ability to swim because, unlike us, they don't have to learn any special strokes to do it. As soon as they can no longer feel the ground beneath their paws, they instinctively do the right thing: They paddle forward with all fours, as if they were running. But dogs don't know that. Get your dog to try it by making a game of it. Incidentally, although water dogs like Newfoundlands or Labradors are known for having webbed feet, all dogs have this trait. Feel your dog's feet—the webbing between the toes is simply a bit more pronounced in some breeds than in others.

A vest for avid swimmers

In principle, every dog should be able to go into the water if she enjoys it. Of course, you need to observe a few safety precautions in order to avoid dangerous situations. Dogs cannot budget their energy sensibly. They romp, run, and swim as long as they can. On land, they can usually just lie down to take a break.

That doesn't work in the water, where the dog may sense too late that she doesn't have enough strength to make it back to shore. And even dogs can get muscle cramps! In order to prevent an accident, don't throw too far or too often when you play fetch, and keep a close eye on your dog. If she is swimming along with you, you should increase your distance very gradually and always stay near the shore. Also, beware of undertows in the water, which can be dangerous for both people and dogs. That's why you should be especially cautious in unfamiliar waters and take no risks. A game of fetch with a floating dummy is tremendous fun for the dog, even if she only gets her paws wet. If you would like to go swimming with your dog regularly, play it safe and get a doggy life vest (available in the pet store). An investment in quality definitely pays off here. High-quality life vests are usually very durable. People who regularly do water work with their dogs always recommend putting a life vest on the animal. If your dog accompanies you for water sports like sailing, surfing, or kayaking, a vest like this is a must anyway. Incidentally, a collar or harness has no business on a dog when she's swimming. There is too great a danger that she'll get a paw stuck in it while she's paddling around, or it will catch on something, like a submerged branch.

Safe shore games

When you take a trip to the shore, be sure to pack the dog's life vest in case she's going to be doing more than just playing on the beach. Respect her natural fear of the waves, and don't chase her into the water.

By the way, most dogs don't like the taste of salty seawater. In case your dog does, don't let her drink too much of it. If you'll be staying at the shore for

What a blast!: Most dogs love playing in the water more than anything, provided they have been introduced slowly and carefully to the wet stuff. Try it yourself to see if your dog is a water rat.

1. Good for the joints and muscles: The beneficial effect of aquatic exercise is even used in physical therapy for dogs, for example, to treat arthritis patients or as rehabilitation after surgery.

2. Always play it safe: Dogs can't budget their energy when they swim. That's why they should never be left unsupervised. In unfamiliar waters, it's better to stay on the shore with your four-legged friend.

a while, you should always bring along plenty of fresh water so that your beach bum can quench her thirst. A shower rinses the salt out of her coat before it can irritate her skin.

Good for the bones

Swimming is healthy. Water games are even used to treat many disorders of the musculoskeletal system in dogs.

Even older dogs can still go into the water and enjoy aquatic sports without worry. A life vest for your dog ensures that nothing will spoil her fun.

Horseback Riding with Your Dog

What this trains: Your dog's stamina and condition.

What you need: Long line, a bicycle as a substitute horse for practicing, leash, and treats.

Many horseback riders are also dog owners—or would like to be—and dream of glorious horseback rides as a threesome. But before you get to that point, some careful training is necessary because the situation is a very special one: You must have not only the horse under control, but your dog as well, even though you can't influence him directly as you usually do.

The right type
A dog's suitability as a horseback trail dog is not determined by breed alone. The dog's individual physical and mental aptitude is the deciding factor.

The ideal is an athletic dog in good physical condition (which means he accompanies you effortlessly and willingly (!) on two- or three-hour walks), not too timid, who can curb his prey drive—if he has it. This addresses the most important characteristic: Your dog should be good at following you and know a few basic signals. It's best to take a young dog on short, 15-minute trips only (provided he is far enough along in his basic obedience training); for longer rides, the dog must be fully grown.

Practice basic obedience with the bicycle
The most important commands that your dog should know around the horse are *sit*, *down*, *stay* or *wait*, *heel* (walk by your leg reliably), and a release word such as *all done*. It goes without saying that you must be able to call him back to you reliably at any time. If he obeys these basic obedience commands when you go for a walk together, that does not mean everything will work equally well when you're on horseback. You can simulate a comparable training situation with the bicycle. Or, you can simply sit someplace high (on a bench or a tree stump) and try out the signals from there.

Trust between horse and dog
The first step to a reliable trail dog is a trusting relationship between the two animals, horse and dog, that is based on respect and experience.

Take your puppy along with you often to the riding stable, and let him get acquainted with the very special smells and noises there. For his first face-to-face encounters with a horse, the

A good team: When dog, horse, and rider have trained well together, there's nothing nicer for the three of them than a relaxed ride out in the country.

puppy should be on the leash and at a safe distance. Caution! Never let your dog run around unattended in the riding stable until he learns which areas are safe for him.

If you want to get an older dog used to horses and riders, you could walk along with a few friends on horseback. Only get as close to horse and rider as your dog will go without hesitation, and act as if this is nothing out of the ordinary. Well-meaning reassurances will only make your dog suspect that there's something fishy about this situation. Your dog should learn to accept the horse as perfectly natural.

Special training with assistance

Eventually, you want to get the dog used to riding in open country. To do this, start a training program with the help of another person. If you train regularly, this can take several weeks, but it's the most reliable method. In the beginning, go along on foot with horse and dog until both animals are accustomed to each other and neither one is afraid of the other. Then, practice riding slowly with the dog on a leash and with a long line (first, though, carefully get the horse used to the leash and the long line; he could be frightened by the snake-like movements); later on, have the dog heel off-leash.

Participating Despite Handicaps

Dog sports provide a wonderful opportunity for people with handicaps to have fun and get some exercise with their four-legged friends.

When Karlos is out with his master, Günter Baumer, the two are never alone: Günter is a paraplegic and has been confined to a wheel chair for 20 years, so he is always accompanied by an aide. A total of six assistants take turns caring for the 38-year-old man, even during walks or recreational activities. Nevertheless, Karlos knows beyond a doubt that only one person is boss here, and that's Master Günter. Günter Baumer and his Briard, a French herding dog, have been together for six years. The software developer fell in love with the breed while visiting the English Garden in Munich, Germany, and nothing could make him change his mind, neither the dog's size—Karlos is 27 inches (68 cm) tall and weighs 103 pounds (47 kg)—nor the fact that herding dogs need plenty of exercise. It had to be this dog and no other. Following the advice of the breeder, Günter Baumer chose a puppy whose temperament would be most compatible with him and his unique situation. "Right from the beginning, Karlos was a very calm and collected fellow, and he's still that way today."

Naturally, the dog needs a lot of exercise and activity because herding dogs demand a lot from their environment, which usually can't offer them their original job—guarding a herd. Therefore, Günter attended a puppy school and other training classes with Karlos right from the start, and, eventually, he also decided to take up a canine sport with his big male Briard: Once a week, they go to obedience class. One of the aides accompanies the

Training together is fun for both: Günter Baumer and his male Briard Karlos practice the exercise "Take a Bow," which they learned in their obedience course. For the dog, there is no question who's boss. He simply adjusts to his master's unique situation as a matter of course. The pair have been attending classes together at the dog school for six years.

pair and assumes responsibility for the exercises that Günter, because of his handicap, cannot carry out himself: *come* or *heel* on the leash, for example. Yet many other elements covered in the course present no problem for Günter, for instance, "Go Backward," "Take a Bow," "Put Away the Toy," and "Find the Treat Bag." Back home, they continue practicing diligently—right now, the two are training Karlos's nose with "Find the Scented Towel."

Dog trainer Anja Mack, who has been with the pair for six years, vouches for the bond between them: "Although other people do work with the dog, Günter is the boss as far as he is concerned.

That is due primarily to Günter's clarity and consistency in dealing with Karlos." Günter Baumer is certain that weekly obedience classes and practicing at home provide an ideal opportunity for keeping his Briard mentally active.

"Many more people with handicaps should take advantage of the opportunity to interact naturally with a dog and participate in dog sports offered by dog schools and clubs, because integration is often much less difficult than you might think," says Günter Baumer. In principle, dog sports like agility or carting are also possible, depending on which limitations a person has to deal with. However, the availability of canine sports for people with handicaps is still limited, although more and more dog schools and clubs are now offering programs specifically for this group.

Tasks that Günter Baumer can't do himself because of his handicap—his arms don't allow him to throw far—are taken over by an aide, who is always there on walks and even at obedience class. The dog isn't confused by the changing roles, because his master decides who belongs to the pack and can give him orders. For Karlos, the dog school classes he attends with his master provide both training and an outlet for his energy.

Thank you—mission accomplished: The many activities that Günter Baumer and his dog have learned and now actively pursue have forged a strong bond between the two. They have become a fantastic team.

125

The Right Sport for Every Dog

Dogs are multitalented. Their love of activity and togetherness and their willingness to learn are the basis for a wide and varied range of sports that offer something for everyone, whether large or small, young or old, purebred or mixed breed. Fun is guaranteed once dog and owner discover the right sport, and the effect on training will be long-lasting. That's because sports bring you closer together. This is especially true of team sports, where it's important to know the strengths and weakness of your teammates—and adapt to them. The sports that we present in the following pages all require teams composed of at least two members. Several dog-handler pairs can also form larger teams and compete with each other for points and prizes. Canine sports, when done properly, encourage both a shared bond between you and your four-legged friend as well as a friendly spirit of fair play in the group. The games suggested earlier can give you an idea of what will appeal to your dog. If he loves dynamic games like "Weave Through My Legs" (❯ pages 56/57), agility might be just right for him. If it turns out he has a great sense of smell (❯ pages 48/49), tracking or search and rescue could be his thing. In any case, the games are good preparation for canine sports.

Fun Comes First in Sports, Too

In the last 20 years, the field of canine sports has grown so rapidly that a comprehensive overview is difficult. Many trendy sports from countries throughout the world have now become established or are finding an ever-growing community of fans—like flyball (❯ pages 136/137) from the United States, obedience (❯ page 144) from Great Britain, or dog pulling sports (❯ pages 156/157) from Switzerland and Austria. The physical demands these sports make on human and animal vary so greatly that even the less athletic participants, two-legged and four-legged alike, can have a good time. In obedience, for instance, the exercises mainly require concentration and cooperation on the part of the dog, combined with a few athletic elements that will not overtax a healthy animal; human handlers have it even easier, because their role is limited to the mentally challenging task of teaching their dogs the required exercises so that they carry them out precisely and cheerfully later on. Similarly, in search and rescue (❯ pages 142/143) and tracking (❯ pages 148/149) their primary function is to assist the dogs skillfully in performing the sport or to cultivate the dogs' abilities so that they can put them to use in carrying out the assigned tasks.

From hurdles to search and rescue

If you like lots of action and have a dog who is happy to go along with your athletic ambitions, you may decide on agility (❯ pages 130/133), turnierhundesport (❯ pages 154/155), canine freestyle (❯ pages 140/141), or disc dog competitions (❯ pages 134/135). Here, both team members are actively involved in the sport, sometimes jumping over hurdles or running through weave poles, sometimes moving together harmoniously in time to the music, or sometimes throwing and catching a flying disc while running at breakneck speed.

This demands both physical and mental effort: It is always important to train and assess the temperament, motivation, and agility of the dog correctly so that he participates in the sport playfully, skillfully, and willingly. For those who love the unusual, canine sports offer plenty to choose from. However, they frequently require a greater commitment of time and money than simple recreational activities with your dog. Included here are sled dog racing (❯ pages 152/153) and its variations, which can be done even without a dog team. These are classified under the heading "Nordic style" and include sports like pulka driving or skijoring.

EXPERT TIP

Canine Good Citizen Test (CGC)

The Canine Good Citizen (CGC) Program is an award program developed by the American Kennel Club (AKC) (❯ Information, page 188); designed to teach basic obedience, it is a good introduction to further training. In the ten-step CGC Test, owner and dog complete a series of exercises that evaluate the dog's social skills, obedience, and ability to behave in public. These include: accepting a friendly stranger; sitting for petting; appearance and grooming; walking on a loose leash; walking through a crowd; *sit, down,* and *stay* on command; coming when called; reaction to another dog; reaction to distractions; and supervised separation. The dog should be at least one year old before taking the test; the test can be repeated at any time.

In addition, owners of dogs who love to run can choose from dog pulling sports like bikejoring, scootering, and canicross (❯ pages 156/157), in which one or two dogs are harnessed in front of a bicycle, scooter, or jogger. Finally, dog sports have joined in a beneficial way with the human desire to help others: Canine search and rescue work (❯ pages 150/151) is physically and mentally demanding as well as time-consuming for both dog and handler. In return, it provides an opportunity to participate in a multifaceted and meaningful activity with the dog, one that more and more dog owners find fascinating.

Training for healthy success

There are a wide variety of dog sports to choose from and almost as many different opportunities to participate in them. Professional instruction and regular training are always advisable. Even the occasional game of Frisbee with your dog, played without lofty ambitions, will benefit from a few lessons; in addition to showing you the correct technique for throwing the disc, they will teach you how to keep your dog healthy and motivated. For instance, you can learn and practice in one of the many dog training schools and canine sports clubs that now offer many sports along with puppy classes and training courses. In the classes, which usually meet once a week, you and your dog will learn correct techniques and a sensible training program. When choosing a dog school, you need to trust your instincts and take a good look at the students: Naturally, you and the trainer must be on the same wavelength, and dogs as well as owners should always look happy and motivated when working together. Many dog schools also offer little fun competitions at which participants can show what they have learned. Here, the emphasis is on having a good time, according to the motto: "The most important thing is not to win, but to take part."

Competing through clubs

Not infrequently, this has led to stirrings of ambition in quite a few dog owners. Then, you have to think about whether you should aim higher and possibly participate in competitions with official tests and regulations. To do this, membership in one of the many canine sports clubs or associations may be required (❯ Information, page 188). Here, trainers work with their two-legged and four-legged students in accordance with specific training guidelines and, given the necessary ambition and commitment, guide them on to championships at the regional, state, national, and even international level.

 PRACTICAL TIP

Always leave the field in a good mood

Reaching goals in canine sporting events along with his master is fun for a dog—provided human ambition doesn't push the dog beyond his limits in the process. Actually, it's always the dog owners who make mistakes, either because their own technique is not (yet) perfect or because they expect too much of their dog. That's why self-criticism and careful observation of your four-legged teammate are essential in canine sports. If the dog appears less and less focused, that should be a sign that maybe it's time to take a break from training. The most important rule: Always leave the field in a good mood, even when the result wasn't so great. Your four-legged teammate certainly deserves that much. Once a dog is frustrated, it's hard to motivate him again.

In almost all competitions, dogs of all breeds as well as mixed breeds are allowed to participate (the World Agility Championship, however, is only for purebred dogs).

Depending on the sport, your dog may need to be a minimum age before he begins training or competing; this could be 15 to 18 months old to compete at the lowest level. Your dog should also have all the necessary vaccinations and be tattooed or microchipped.

Dog owners who choose these more demanding canine sports usually invest considerably more time than what it takes for the more fun-oriented sports training at a dog school. They train several times a week and frequently go to competitions on the weekends, either to participate themselves or to see how good the others are. The quest for success, however, is a purely human characteristic; that's why in dog sports your motto should always be "fair play before ambition." Your four-legged teammate's health and state of mind are of prime importance for training and participation in competitions.

You dog couldn't care less how many trophies there are on the mantelpiece at home. He just wants to have fun participating in a sport with you and know that you are happy and pleased with him—with no pressure to perform and no winner's circle.

Totally focused: Concentrating intently, the Dalmatian runs through the weave poles. It's not as easy as it looks at first glance, but the dog loves this athletic challenge.

Agility for Large and Small

What this trains: Condition, stamina, concentration, harmony, and teamwork.

What you need: Toys and/or treats for training; the dog should have mastered basic obedience training.

Hardly any other dog sport has experienced such a groundswell of enthusiasm in recent years as the agility course for dogs and their human partners. Perhaps, that's because it satisfies so many needs at once: The dog gets to run and jump, and while he's having fun, he demonstrates what we regard as his most outstanding skill—the ability to cooperate closely with his human teammate. At the same time, he is out there along with other dog-human teams and, when everything is relaxed and fair, gets lots of praise and encouragement from his master. Handlers, in turn, experience tremendous closeness with their dogs while training

obedience and teamwork; furthermore, they get to participate in a sport and have to face challenges themselves. With this combination of physical and mental work, you can hardly call agility a mere pastime.

The tasks sound easy at first and often look almost effortless at agility trials: As in some equestrian events, the dog has to tackle a variety of obstacles in a specific order while his handler usually runs along beside him and directs him through the course.

You'll soon realize how much skill and, above all, what teamwork it takes for dog and handler to do this, if you try it once with your dog. Most dog schools and canine sports club offer introductory courses—but be careful: it's addictive!

Even little dogs do great things here

Almost all dogs can take part in agility because this sport—depending on your goals—can easily be adapted to the constitution of each dog or person. Even if the dog has a physical handicap, this need not prevent him from participating (❯ "Dogs with handicaps" page 158). As a result, you'll encounter dogs of (almost) every size and shape on the course, because the obstacles themselves come in different sizes, or they can be adjusted so that even toy breeds like Papillions, Shih Tsu, and Chihuahuas, or very small mixed breeds can take part in agility events.

Only very large dogs (or short-legged dogs with long backs) have difficulty with the jumps and turns that agility demands of them. However, if

Tunnel: The Sheltie shoots through the tunnel like lightning. What looks so effortless here is the result of carefully introducing each obstacle and getting the dog used to it.

the obstacles in question are simply omitted, even these dogs can run the course without endangering their health.

This fast-moving, dynamic sport is not suitable for dogs with disorders of the musculoskeletal system (such as hip dysplasia, osteochondrosis dissecans, or arthritis), cardiovascular disease, or other ailments that would prohibit physical stress.

The twists and turns of the course

A typical agility course is about 100 to 200 yards (100–200 m) long and consists of ten to twenty obstacles, for example: single jumps, double jumps, and panel jumps—the dog jumps over these obstacles; a broad jump or long jump consisting of several individual sections placed an equal distance apart—the dog has to clear this obstacle in a single bound; a tire jump (the tire can be raised or lowered) that the dog jumps through; a flexible tunnel, which can be set up in one or more curves, and a

tunnel with a fabric tube on one end that the dog has to push up as he runs through it; the A-frame, an obstacle shaped like a little roof, which the dog has to climb up and run down again; a seesaw or teeter, which the dog has to tip by skillfully shifting his weight so that he can run down the other side again; a dog walk, similar to a balance beam, which the dog has to walk across without losing his balance; a pause table—the dog has to jump up on it and remain there for five seconds before he can continue; and the weave poles, which consists of 12 poles placed a specific distance apart that the dog has to zigzag through.

Some obstacles, like the dog walk, the A-frame, and the seesaw, have a so-called contact zone at the beginning and end that is colorfully marked. An important rule says that the dog has to touch the contact zone at each end with at least one paw when entering and leaving the obstacle. A second rule states that the dog and handler must tackle the obstacles in a specific sequence, not crisscross the course however they please.

World champion on six legs

The requirement that dog and handler run through the course in a specific order addresses an important task of the handler. He must use verbal and body signals to make sure the dog stays on course, touches the contact zones, remains on the pause table for the prescribed time, enters the weave poles with the left shoulder and doesn't skip any poles, jumps over the hurdles from the correct side, and so on.

 PRACTICAL TIP

"Agility course" in your backyard

You can even set up a little obstacle course in the backyard using simple objects. For instance, a broom handle placed across two low stools or through two milk crates makes a hurdle for the dog to jump over (better too low than too high). Put a few sticks in the ground the right distance apart to create a weave pole obstacle. Pet stores carry many styles of fabric tunnels the dog can run through. A balance beam made from two sturdy boxes and a wooden board trains the dog's sense of balance and agility. Perhaps you have an old rubber tire somewhere that can be attached right and left to a branch with a rope; this makes a great piece of equipment to test your dog's enthusiasm for jumping. Important: Make sure everything is safe, securely mounted, and never too high.

Each obstacle is trained individually, at first, until the dog has mastered it fearlessly and flawlessly. When they run through the course together, another challenge facing the human half of the team quickly becomes apparent: The handler must always be careful not to stand in the dog's way and must indicate the correct direction with body signals, because in addition to navigating all obstacles faultlessly, speed counts.

It's not uncommon for agility to start out as a pleasant hobby and, then, develop into an ambitious sport with competitive events that go all the way to the world championship, where pairs or teams compete against each other.

To level the playing field and, thus, give all participants an equal chance, entrants are divided into levels based on size and ability. Depending on the height of the dog at the shoulder—there are different classes for dogs measuring from less than 11 inches (28 cm) to more than 22 inches (56 cm)—the height of the jumps varies from 4 inches (10 cm) to 26 inches (66 cm). Levels of competition range from Novice to Excellent.

The course is easy for novices and, then, gets increasingly harder and longer. There is also a seniors class for older dogs. Then there are "Jumpers," courses with no contact obstacles, where the most important thing is speed.

Incidentally, the best sports are not always the human-dog teams who consistently finish first, but rather those who live by the motto: "The most important thing is not to win but to take part." Even in competition, the fun of doing something together and the health of your canine teammate should always come first.

1. Seesaw: Agility is suitable for dogs of all sizes. A Dachshund runs in a class for small dogs. The obstacles here are set lower than in classes for larger dogs.

2. A-frame: In contact obstacles, an important rule states that the dog must touch the painted areas at the beginning and end with at least one paw.

Weave poles: Spectacular and very training-intensive. It takes a lot of practice before a dog can zigzag through the poles nimbly.

Jumping over obstacles: Agility as a competitive sport is only for dogs that are in tip-top shape. That's why the dog needs a thorough physical exam from the veterinarian before beginning agility.

Disc Dog Competitions—a Sport with Crowd Appeal

What this trains: Concentration, coordination, and stamina.

What you need: Good agility and condition and flying discs made especially for dogs. There are protective vests for elite athletes that protect the handler's upper body when the dog does back vaults.

This spectacular sport is always a good show-stopper. Dog and handler demonstrate their skill in displays lasting just one or two minutes.

Different disciplines are involved here. In the so-called "Mini-Distance," time is what matters most: The dog tries to catch as many discs thrown by his human partner as possible in 60 or 90 seconds (depending on the rules). The playing field measures about 20×50 yards (18×46 m) and has a throwing line and different throwing areas. The thrower stands on the throwing line and has just one disc. The dog has to bring it back to the thrower after each throw. If he doesn't, the thrower can go onto the playing field to get the disc. Natu-

rally, that means lost time. There are points for every disc the dog catches, depending on the throw distance (maximum of 50 yards [46 m]). In the "Long Distance," it's not speed that's important, but rather the length of the throw: Every human-dog team has three throws from a starting line. The winner is the team with the longest throw caught by a dog.

In "Freestyle," it's not just speed and distance that count, but many other elements as well, making this event the most spectacular in the sport. Here, human and dog can get creative. In a performance lasting less than two minutes and set to music they have chosen themselves, they perform an original routine consisting of throws and tricks that demand skill and athleticism from both team members. Often, special costumes for the handler and the circus-quality acrobatics of dog and human alike make these choreographed performances a real crowd-pleaser: for example, when the handler lies on his back, throws the disc through his legs, and the dog dives after it; or when the dog uses the handler's body as a takeoff ramp. For moves like this, the handler can even wear a protective vest to avoid getting scratched by the dog's nails.

A demanding sport

For disc dog competitions, both human and dog have to be in good physical condition and possess athletic ability. Consequently, the sport is only suitable for fully grown dogs in excellent health.

In any case, dog owners should have their dogs examined thoroughly by a veterinarian before participating in this sport (❯ page 166). In principle, every dog can become a disc dog, if he is sufficiently motivated and fit. It takes skill for the human teammate to match throws and jumps to the size and ability of the dog. Disc dog requires not only physical condition, but also cleverness. This high-speed sport has a growing number of followers here and abroad. Workshops and seminars offer opportunities to train (❯ Information, page 188), because proper know-how and a sensible training program are essential in order to participate responsibly in this sport.

 PRACTICAL TIP

Frisbee for fun

Even if you don't have competitive ambitions, playing Frisbee with your dog is fun—provided you follow a few rules: Standard Frisbee discs are not suitable for games with your dog. They are usually too hard and can splinter. Pet stores carry special discs made just for dogs. Typical beginners' mistake: You throw the disc straight at the dog. If you do that, you're too likely to risk injuring the dog. Correct: Throw the disc away from the dog, starting with throws that are nearly horizontal and travel only a short distance. Only practice twice a day for five minutes at a time, like champion athlete Jochen Schleicher. He introduced disc dog to Europe in the mid-1990s. His tip: "Stop when it's going great, and then put the disc away. That way the game stays exciting for the dog."

1. Throw correctly: Pros have mastered different throwing techniques. The most important rule: Never throw the disc straight at the dog. Start with short throws, then, gradually increase the distance and height.

2. Frisbee master: Spectacular leaps like this are only for healthy, well-trained disc dogs. Stick with discs made especially for dogs, even for recreational use.

Flyball—A Game of Skill

What this trains: Good physical condition and stamina, eagerness to retrieve, and discipline.

What you need: Lots of balls; naturally, they should be the right size and type for the four-legged flyballer.

This high-speed dog sport also originated in the United States—in California, to be precise, where a devoted owner devised a ball machine to keep his energetic dog occupied. When the dog stepped on a pedal, a ball flew up out of the box about ten feet (3 m) into the air and the dog had to catch it. The game quickly caught on with other dog owners, and the canine sport of flyball was born. Techniques and rules have changed a lot since then, but one thing has remained: What's most important is that the dogs have fun satisfying their need for activity and their love of retrieving. This addresses an important misconception right away: The best candidates for this running and jumping sport

are not ball-crazy dogs, but rather those who will bring back the ball reliably, in other words, retrieve it.

Team sport with active dogs

In this activity, the human teammates play a very easy part: Their job is primarily to be trainers and coaches rather than fellow runners, as in agility (❯ page 130), or even acrobats, as in disc dog (❯ pages 134/135). For this reason, the condition of the dog owner is less important than the dog's aptitude, fitness, and willingness to cooperate. In this sport, the dog has to jump over four hurdles without help from her handler, then trigger the release mechanism on the flyball box, catch the ball in her mouth as it flies out, and bring it back over the four hurdles to the start/finish line again. In contrast to the early days of flyball, today the ball no longer shoots up into the air, but travels more horizontally so that the dog is not required to make any high leaps.

Clear rules for fair play

Competitively, flyball is played as a team sport today. It works like this: Two teams, each made up of four dogs and four handlers, line up on adjacent flyball courses. Clear rules for competition guarantee that the playing conditions are fair.

The height of the hurdles (from a minimum of about 8 inches [20 cm] to a maximum of 16 inches [40 cm]) is determined by the smallest dog on each team. In addition, the teams have to report a sort of best time, according to in which different division

1. Trigger the release mechanism: Whether at a competitive level or not, a growing number of dog schools and clubs offer flyball today. Amy, a Beauceron, practices using the flyball box.

2. The ball flies out: With both front paws, she steps on a pedal mechanism that flings out a ball. Now her task is to catch the ball deftly in her mouth.

they are placed. If a team beats this reference time by at least half a second, the race is not counted. This prevents a fast team from deliberately putting themselves in a slower class in order to clean up the prizes at that level. As simple as this sport looks, it demands a lot of discipline and willingness to cooperate on the part of the dog, whereas the handler must be able to motivate the dog and correctly assess her stamina and fitness. For players who would like to compete, a thorough health check by the veterinarian before participating is a must here, too.

3. Catch the ball: With the ball in her mouth, she now has to return to the start/finish line, jumping over four hurdles along the way. For many dogs, staying on course is not easy.

Motivation is Everything!

"On your marks, get set, go!" In the next game or sporting
event, your four-legged friend will start out highly motivated,
if you get him into the right mood with a few little tricks.
Then, his enthusiasm will usually be boundless.

1 **Exciting start signal to start:** If you practice a
sport with your dog, think up an encouraging signal
for the start of every round. A short, snappy *"Let's
go!"* or *"We're off!"* tells the dog that it's time for
action. You don't have to shout it, but it should
always sound the same and be really motivating—
that makes the activity exciting for your dog and
helps him to concentrate fully on you and the
course.

2 **Play a little game occasionally:** You can make
great use of the waiting period before the next
round to perk up your teammate. Take along his
favorite toy and throw it a few times, or have a
little tug-of-war—and keep varying the games! That
energizes your dog and keeps his attention focused
on you.

3 **Gourmet rewards:** If your dog knows that you
always bring along very special treats when the
two of you play games or participate in sports,
he's guaranteed to be more enthusiastic than if
he only gets the usual dry kibble. You're sure to
know what your dog really goes for; maybe it's
cheese cubes, cooked bits of chicken or liver, or
jerky. Or you can try preparing a gourmet treat,
perhaps a firm pancake made with ground liver
or cooked bits of chicken that can be cut up into
little pieces.

4 **Pay attention:** Say you send your dog to "Find
the Treat Bag" (❯ page 38), and while he's supposed
to be hunting around in the field, you carry on a
lively conversation with another dog owner: Your
dog will notice that you're not paying attention to
him. That's not the way to keep him motivated! Stay
focused on the task at hand. Then, you'll be able to
tell right away if your dog's spirits begin to flag.
Depending on the length of the game or sport, end
it then on a high note or play a motivational game.

5 **Keep it exciting:** Dogs react instinctively to
movement. Take advantage of that by making yourself interesting for your four-legged friend. If he is
supposed to bring something back to you but has a
hard time giving up his booty, walk backward while
calling him to you. Hop back and forth or run away
from him for a short distance. If you want to focus
his attention on a specific object, pick it up and play
with it enthusiastically; then, the object will be
attractive for the dog, too.

6 **Stop when you're having fun:** Too many repetitions are a real motivation killer. Conclude an exercise or a step in a game before your four-legged
teammate has a chance to get tired of it. Frequent
short practices that are lots of fun produce better
results than long sessions that take too much out of
your dog.

Canine **Freestyle**—Dancing With Your Dog

What this trains: Agility, concentration, and cooperation.

What you need: Music, clicker, target stick (❯ pages 40/64), and props like a hat or scarf; for performances, dancing clothes or costumes.

You can participate in this popular sport throughout the year, regardless of wind and weather, because you can practice with your dog on the lawn just as well as in the living room. And, you always decide for yourself which moves you want to rehearse, because in canine freestyle, you can let your imagination run wild!

A sport with plenty of variety

Moving along with a partner in time to the music is a good activity for any dog. Even older dogs or those with health problems can participate, because the program can be tailored precisely to their abilities. In canine freestyle, also called dog dancing, the most

important thing is to have fun exercising together. However, participants in this dog sport also pay a great deal of attention to competition, and, then, what counts with the judges and audience are creativity and harmonious teamwork. Accompanied by music, dog and human present a series of rehearsed moves and tricks that often have their roots in the canine sport of obedience (❯ pages 144/145), from which dog dancing has developed as a sort of freestyle variation.

With tricks and props

To start with, each element of the exercise is trained separately, for example, with a clicker or target stick (❯ pages 40/64). Pushing and pulling the dog in order to get her into a certain position is taboo here, as in all dog sports. Classical elements in canine freestyle are moves like "Weave Through My Legs" (❯ pages 56/57), "Jump Through My Legs" (❯ pages 82/83), or "Jump Through My Arms" (❯ pages 74/75), paw tricks, going backward, foot positions, "Twist" (❯ pages 80/81), and working with props. Here, too, there are no limits to your creativity, provided you don't endanger the dog or demand too much of her. Tricks using a hat, scarf, or handbag belonging to the human dance partner's costume are all possible. Ultimately, the choreography is a combination of all rehearsed elements—heelwork and tricks—that the dog carries out in time to the music at the dancer's verbal signals and/or gestures.

1. Freestyle with costume: Competitions focus on two styles: "Musical Freestyle" and "Heelwork to Music." Judges award points based on things like the number of figures, harmonious interaction, motivation of the dog, and, naturally, creativity of the choreography.

2. Training at any time: Whether indoors or out, you can train the individual elements of the canine freestyle at any time with your dog.

3. For young and old: Many young people enjoy this creative sport—there are special courses for them—but older dog owners like to dance along, too.

141

Searching for Missing Persons

What this trains: Sense of smell, concentration, cooperation, and discipline.

What you need: Tracking harness, special leash, someone who will hide, articles with that person's scent, rewards (a game and/or treats), and clothespins or colored tape to mark the trail.

In no other canine sport is the dog's terrific sense of smell showcased so impressively as in the search for a missing person. The dog is taught to follow the individual scent of a person and not just, as in tracking, the traces that the person has left behind on the ground (❯ pages 48/49).

Well-trained dogs can detect an individual scent trail, which is as unique as a fingerprint, even after several days, and not just in field and forest, but even on asphalt, in towns, in buildings, and so on— and they can follow it for several miles (kilometers). It takes a lot of training to develop this ability. The reward for all the effort and years of training comes when dog and owner are called upon in an emergency. Trained search dogs are often used by the police and search and rescue teams to find missing persons.

Although there are still no standardized tests for searching, some training institutions and search and rescue services have their own certification tests.

Demanding work

The training demands a great deal of concentration and discipline, and not just from the dog.

In order to teach the dog how to trail and follow him as he does it (which always requires a special tracking harness and long leash) without disturbing him, the handler must know how to use the leash and be adept at interpreting the dog's body language. When used professionally, the dog is allowed to sniff a scent article belonging to the missing person, for example, a sock. Then he picks up the scent himself and follows the trail. When he does this, he doesn't just keep his nose to the ground (as in tracking), but also lifts his head in order to pick up the scent of the missing person (air scenting). Searching is a very demanding pursuit for both dog and handler.

1. Totally focused: Searching is a dog sport that forges a bond between dog and handler, because teamwork is essential in order to reach the goal—finding the missing person.

2. Follow the scent trail: In searching, the skill of the handler lies in interpreting the dog's body language correctly and staying out of his way as he follows the trail.

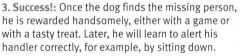

3. Success!: Once the dog finds the missing person, he is rewarded handsomely, either with a game or with a tasty treat. Later, he will learn to alert his handler correctly, for example, by sitting down.

Obedience—A Highly Disciplined Sport

What this trains: Concentration, cooperation, discipline, and body control.

What you need: Leash, clicker, target stick (❯ pages 40/64), and treats and toys as rewards; for professional training, equipment like traffic cones, wooden dumbbells, and hurdles.

The word obedience barely conveys what a multifaceted and demanding sport this is for dog and owner alike. Like agility (❯ pages 130/131), obedience originated in England, where it has a huge following and is carried out at many competitions. In North America, too, obedience enjoys growing popularity as a competitive sport. Different organizations have their own rules and regulations governing obedience trials.

Yet, the individual elements of obedience training are not just for competitions; they are also ideal activities for everyday, indoors or outdoors, all year-round.

As with all the activities presented in this book, the most important rule in obedience training is that you get the dog to cooperate through positive reinforcement, never by grabbing, pushing, pulling, or even punishment.

Discipline without drills

In obedience, dog and handler perform different exercises in perfect harmony; that means, they have to be carried out quickly, precisely, and cheerfully by the dog. Essential training elements of the individual exercises sound rather mundane at first: heel, stay, recall, retrieve, directed exercises, scent discrimination, temperament tests, and social behavior toward other dogs and people. But it's what the dog-human teams do with these elements that is fascinating and never ceases to amaze the audience, especially because obedience is a very quiet dog sport: The signals are given softly and with the smallest of gestures.

The difficulty of obedience exercises varies depending on the class. Perfection plays a major role in obedience, yet, it can be learned playfully, because even in this sport, the fun of doing something together is what counts most. Naturally, rewarding the dog with treats and games is an important part of training (❯ "Ready for the trial," page 146). The clicker and target stick are often used in training obedience (❯ pages 40/64).

Pass it on: During an obedience trial, the ring steward lets the handler know which command to give the dog—here it's *sit*.

 EXPERT TIP

Early Success

You can even practice simple obedience exercises with a puppy, and once your dog is old enough, he can compete in the Novice Class at the American Kennel Club's obedience trials. Exercises for this level include: heel on-leash, heel off-leash, figure eight, stand for examination, recall, long sit (1 minute), and long down (3 minutes). The dog can only advance to the next level once he has earned a certain number of points; however, you can compete again in a level as often as you like. In subsequent levels, the exercises get longer and harder.

Even with handicaps

Obedience is especially versatile because it really is suitable for every dog. Even certain health problems don't have to be an obstacle. And, because here, unlike in agility or canine freestyle, the handler does not have to move along with the dog, training is less physically challenging; instead, a sensible training program emphasizes brainwork.

That's why it's not at all unusual to meet older participants as well as people with handicaps in competitions; it's even possible to do obedience from a wheelchair (❯ page 124).

Something for everyone

When you watch obedience pros during a competition, you almost get the impression that the dogs are being guided by remote control, so precisely and promptly do they carry out the signals. And, yet, the dogs are highly motivated and romp happily with their owners when their turns are over and they get rewarded with a few minutes of free play.

If you would like to find out if you and your four-legged partner are capable of this much precision, many canine sports clubs and dog schools will give you the opportunity. Training methods often vary greatly. Sometimes it is play oriented, sometimes it focuses more on competition. In many dog schools, obedience training is a mixture of everyday exercises that are quite useful in traffic, in the subway, and in daily interactions with other people, for example, *stay* or *stop* when the dog is in motion, *park* between the owner's legs, or *go backward* (❯ pages 78/79). But training also includes games and tricks like "Go Around the Obstacle" (❯ pages 53/54) or "High Five" (❯ pages 69/70). If you and your dog enjoy working on exercises step by step (and also practice them as part of your daily routine), you'll quickly succeed here and discover an ideal activity that is so varied that you can even do it when your dog is well up in years. If you practice the elements of obedience regularly with your dog, you'll find that it helps you become good teammates: That's because observing your dog closely, interpreting his body language correctly, and understanding his special abilities are essential for achieving the harmony you're seeking.

Discipline: The handler should be in control at all times.

 PRACTICAL TIP

Ready for the trial

Every dog-handler team can participate in obedience trials, regardless of the dog's age, size, or breed.

Several organizations hold obedience trials, including the American Kennel Club (AKC), United Kennel Club (UKC), Australian Shepherd Club of America (ASCA), and Mixed Breed Dog Clubs of America (MBDCA). At obedience trials sponsored by the AKC, the competition is divided into Novice Class, Open Class, and Utility Class.

If you are bitten by the bug and can invest more time than an hour a week at the dog school, it's best to find a club that offers obedience training specifically for those who want to compete in the trials.

What you should know beforehand: You can only participate in the AKC's obedience trials if your dog is registered with the AKC as Purebred Alternative Listing (PAL), which is for purebreds without papers. In addition, your dog should have all the required vaccinations and be microchipped or tattooed.

In an obedience trial, a ring steward announces all exercises to the participants. During the trial, the dog is not allowed to be rewarded with food or a toy (this is only permitted after completion of all exercises, outside the obedience ring).

1. Thank you: Sitting in front of the handler with a metal dumbbell is an exercise for advanced students. According to the rules, the dog has to carry the dumbbell a certain way (by the middle), he may not chew on it, and he must not *drop it* until he gets the command to do so.

2. Wait patiently: The four traffic cones mark off a box that is frequently used in obedience trials. Here, the ring steward has instructed the handler to have the dog stop at a specific marker and *stay* there.

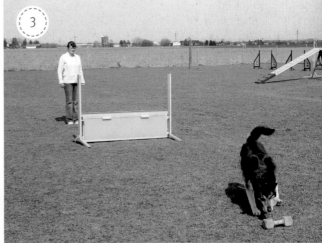

3. There and back again: The dog must remain in the *down* position while his handler throws the dumbbell over the hurdle. Once she is beside him again and gives the signal, he has to retrieve it quickly, jumping over the hurdle once on the way there and once on the way back.

4. Complete concentration: Directed exercises are very challenging for both dog and handler. This dog was put in the *down* position inside the box. When the handler calls him, he must sit facing her and then return to the box at her command.

Tracking for "Super Sleuths"

What this trains: Sense of smell and concentration (❯ "Scent Trail" pages 48/49).

What you need: Tracking harness, leash, a variety of scent articles, something to mark the track, and treats.

A dog who is allowed to follow his nose is completely in his element. Grant him this pleasure by turning it into a fantastic activity for both of you. Working with a tracking dog is especially impressive because—with a little practice—he follows a scent trail that is invisible to us. Yet, that's what makes it difficult to guide him properly in this invisible task. Mistakes can confuse him unnecessarily. So here are a few basic tips for tracking.

Come up with a few rituals

A special harness reserved for tracking is ideal. It does not irritate the dog's sensitive neck as he follows a scent trail, and it distributes pressure better

across his chest. If you always put the harness on just before you go tracking, it also gives the dog a signal for what's about to happen. A second ritual is a verbal command that you use only for tracking, for example, *Find it!* or *Track!*

Lay a track with turns

Once you have practiced following a simple track—one that goes in a straight line for 20 to 30 feet (7–10 m)—three or four times with your dog (❯ "Scent Trail" pages 48/49) and you feel that your dog gets the idea, you can make it harder. For example, you can have the track change direction by turning to the left or right; start with just one turn, then, put in several turns later on. Make sure to mark each of the turns so that you can recognize them later when you're following your dog as he tracks. You can do this by sticking a tracking flag in the ground about 12 inches (30 cm) from the corner where the dog won't notice it. Let the dog start sniffing around, as described. If he follows the change of direction, then everything is wonderful. If not, stop moving when the dog gets a few steps ahead of you. Don't help out with any verbal or visual signals. The dog should have the opportunity to find his way back to the track on his own. Keep a relaxed hold on the leash and don't pull or tug in a particular direction.

Important: Don't stand directly on the corner, because then the dog can't sniff at it. Give him time to sniff in a little circle around the corner, so he can find which way the track goes next. Only when he is really perplexed should you use a hand signal at

1. Ideal terrain: Medium-high grass is perfect for beginners because the ground disturbance that results when you lay the track is easier for the dog to notice, as well as remaining somewhat visible for the handler.

2. Ground work: His nose to the ground, the dog sniffs along the track. His handler follows, holding the leash loosely to avoid disturbing him.

ground level to point out the direction of the next short section, until the dog picks up the scent again. Many dog schools and canine sports clubs now offer this sport. It is suitable for any dog, regardless of breed or size, because our four-legged friends all have fantastic noses! If your dog loves to follow scents, and you would like to let him track competitively, organizations such as the American Kennel Club offer tracking tests where you can do this (❯ Information, page 188).

3. Found it!: It is important to lay an article at both the start and the finish of the track. When the dog reaches the goal, he gets a reward or a game.

Canine **Search and Rescue**

What this trains: Sense of smell, coordination, and concentration. In this work, a very close, trusting bond develops between dog and handler.

What you need: A lot of time for training and a healthy dog who is not too small.

Canine search and rescue is more than just an activity or recreational sport, because the goal of training is not a competition or tournament, but rather an emergency, where human lives are at stake. A classic use for a rescue dog team, consisting of dog and handler, is searching for missing persons, for example, elderly or disoriented people who have lost their way, joggers or recreational horseback riders who have had an accident somewhere out in the country, possible suicides who have disappeared, accident victims who left the scene in a state of shock, and so on. Urban search and rescue dogs, also called disaster dogs, are used in places like earthquake areas. Rescue dogs who are part of mountain rescue teams dig out people who have been buried under avalanches. And, in water rescue, the dogs bring live victims safely to land or find the bodies of those who have drowned.

Four-legged "decathletes"

Training to become a rescue dog team requires several hours a week, and frequently weekends, as well. It takes about two years to pass all the necessary tests and be certified. The dog trains in different disciplines, rather like a decathlete, for example: searching in rubble; surefootedness, which is the ability to negotiate all types of terrain safely; and distance control, which is following commands when far from the handler. The training for the dog is designed so that she enjoys her work and is highly motivated. As a rule, dogs can start training at six to eight months of age; ideally, a dog should be no more than three years old when she begins. The dog handler also has an enormous amount of material to master, starting with first aid and emergency medical care, then canine science, disaster search techniques, air scenting techniques, evaluation of site conditions, map and compass reading, and using emergency rescue equipment.

Wanted: Dogs who love to play

Some breeds are found more frequently than others in search and rescue work, because they often have highly developed abilities as a result of selective breeding.

1. No fear: A rescue dog must deal with a wide variety of situations, including fire. Danger is always present during actual deployment, but dog and handler train together so they will know what to do.

2. Surefooted: Training to become a search and rescue dog team takes about two years. Courses are offered by search and rescue organizations or special clubs. Many of them have introductory courses that allow you to learn about it and try it out.

The ideal dog is medium-sized, loves to play (motivation!), gets along well with others, and is not too timid.

Rewards of the work

A rescue dog team usually works on a voluntary basis; however, some rescue organizations, such as the National Disaster Search Dog Foundation, offer the training free of charge to certain participants. There are other expenditures, though, for example, the cost of traveling long distances to training sites and centers. But the rewards for such an enormous commitment are the trusting relationship that develops between dog and handler and the satisfaction that comes from working as a team to help people in distress.

3. Nose work: One of the primary jobs of a rescue dog is searching for missing persons. In principle, all purebred and mixed-breed dogs above a certain size are suitable for this kind of work.

Sled Dog Racing and Nordic Style

What this trains: In these sports, the emphasis is on the dogs' physical conditioning, teamwork, and willingness to cooperate with their handlers.

What you need: Equipment can be expensive, depending on the sport. For skijoring, the essentials are cross-country skis, a towline, and a special harness for the dog.

Winter sports with dogs are very popular now. That may come as a surprise, especially if you think just of dog sledding, which requires participants to keep a team of dogs. But even owners of one or two dogs can use their four-legged friends as teammates in winter dog sports like pulka driving or skijoring, which fall under the heading "Nordic style."

Nordic style for cross-country skiers

In pulka driving, the cross-country skier is attached by an elastic line to a pulk, which is pulled by a dog harnessed in front of it. The pulk was originally a sort of small wooden toboggan used in Nordic countries to transport provisions or small loads. Today, it is a plastic sled that is loaded with weights, depending on the class. One or two dogs can be hitched in front of a pulk. A competition course is about 7 to 12 miles (12–20 km) long.

Skijoring is done in much the same way, but without the pulk. Here dog and handler are connected directly to each other by a towline that attaches to the dog's harness on one end and his teammate's skijor belt on the other. In competitive skijoring, courses are about 6 to 7 miles (10–12 km) long. In both disciplines, the idea is not to have the dog do all the pulling; instead, the skijorer actively follows the dog. A skillful team will be able to move along together at a good clip, taking the curves in such a way that the skier doesn't leave the track or fall. Nordic style is offered by dog sledding clubs. Training takes place throughout the year, usually without snow and skis, of course, but instead as fitness training when bicycling, hiking, jogging, or swimming.

Sled dog teams

In sled dog races, several dogs are used to pull a sled driven by their human teammate, called a musher.

The musher's task is to guide the sled dog team using only specific voice commands. Competitions are divided into classes based on the number of dogs in the team (from two or three dogs to more than eight). There are sprint, middle, and long distance races; the longest sled dog race in the world is the legendary Alaskan Iditarod, which is about 1,100 miles (1,800 km) long.

Not just for Huskies

Sled dog racing and Nordic style are not just for classic Nordic breeds like the Husky, Alaskan Malamute, Samoyed, or Greenland Dog; many other purebred and mixed-breed dogs can participate as well, provided they are neither too small nor too heavy. Prerequisites are that the dog is in good health and is physically fit (a race veterinarian is present at competitions). The most important factor in determining a dog's suitability for this sport is that he loves to run.

 PRACTICAL TIP

On the trail with your dog

An increasing number of winter sports use specially constructed trails, called loipes, where you can also take your dog (information available from tourist bureaus or local authorities). Introduce untrained dogs very gradually to these winter sports! If your dog is in good condition and you are out with him in the snow for any length of time, you should check his paws regularly and, if necessary, protect them with special barrier creams or booties. It takes most dogs a while to get used to snow boots with Velcro closures, so it's better to try them out in a dry run at home.

A strong team: A sled dog team consists of at least two dogs. In competitions, most teams start in the four-dog class. Driving a sled pulled by more than eight dogs takes superb skill.

Turnierhundesport (THS)

What this trains: Obedience, agility, condition, and the bond between dog and the handler

What you need: Athletic attire, leash, more or less time for training (depending on your goals), and a willingness to join a club.

This relatively new sport originated in Germany, where it is enjoys tremendous popularity. Although it has not yet been officially recognized by the World Canine Organization (Fédération Cynologique International, or FCI), this could change in the near future as it spreads to other countries. It is famous for spectacular scenes of dogs and their handlers performing together with amazing skill. Athletes who set high standards for themselves can realize their dreams here. Yet, even those with more modest ambitions or abilities will find that THS, as this sport is commonly abbreviated, provides plenty of opportunity for participation.

The events

Turnierhundesport comprises several different events. The first is the tetrathlon (*Vierkampf*), which consists of four elements: obedience exercises, hurdles, weave poles, and an obstacle course. The obedience exercises include heeling on-leash and off-leash with turns, tempo changes, and pauses; and sit-from-motion and down-from-motion followed by recalls. The dog must be able to heel, assume a basic position (*sit* by the handler's knee), and sit facing the handler (for example, when recalled from *sit* or *down*). The second element of this four-part competition is the hurdle race. Three hurdles measuring 16 inches (40 cm) high are set up on a course 55 yards (50 m) long; the dog has to jump over these hurdles while her human teammate runs along parallel to her. The third element, the weave poles, is always great for exciting sports photos: Dog and handler run together through seven elastic poles 6 feet (1.8 m) high. It takes good technique to run through the poles together at high speed. In the final element of the tetrathlon, the obstacle course, the dog has to get over eight obstacles (A-frame, tunnel, barrel, hurdle, and so on) while the handler runs along parallel to the obstacle course.

Another event in the THS is the cross-country race. The course can be either 1 or 3 miles (2 or 5 km) in length. The dog runs along on the leash.

The Combination Speed Cup (CSC) is a team event. Three dog-plus-handler teams compete in a sort of relay race consisting of three elements of the tetrathlon: hurdles, weave poles, and obstacle course. What's important here are fast changes,

1. High-speed teamwork: In the obstacle course, the dog has to make it over eight obstacles while her human teammate runs along parallel to her. Here, too, teamwork is important: The competition is timed, and the clock stops only when the last member of the team crosses the finish line.

2. Harmony and technique: In the weave poles, dog and handler run through the poles together. Careful training and good technique are necessary, so that neither teammate gets ahead of the other.

running speed, and technique. The "Shorty" is an abbreviated version of the CSC; here, the course consists of only two sections, and two dog-plus-handler teams compete.

In the Qualification Speed Cup (QSC), two dog-plus-handler teams run simultaneously through two parallel obstacle courses; the victor advances to the next round.

The final event, the obstacle course, is divided into two classes, one for dogs measuring less than 20 inches (50 cm) at the shoulder and one for dogs above this height. The dog has to make it over eight obstacles while the handler runs parallel to her.

Year-round training

The German Kennel Club (see Information) sets the rules for these competitions, and teams of dogs and their handlers can train year-round at member clubs and associations. Purebred and mixed-breed dogs of all sizes are allowed to compete; even children under ten years of age can participate, if they are able to control their dog.

Dog Pulling Sports

···❖ **What this trains:** Condition, coordination, cooperation.

What you need: A special pulling harness, tug line, and cart (different styles are available).

The dog has a long history as a draft animal that goes far beyond sled dogs pulling cargo and passengers across the snow in sub-freezing temperatures. In cities and rural areas everywhere, dogs have been used from time immemorial to transport trade goods, belongings, milk cans, and even people.

Many dogs can do it

Today, the use of powerful dogs for pulling loads is seen mainly in athletic events, especially in Switzerland and Austria, where organized dog pulling sports have long been popular. Yet, whereas a draft

dog was once valued primarily for his ability to work and humane treatment was given scant consideration, pulling sports today focus more on providing large, powerful dogs with an enjoyable activity well suited to their physical stature and temperament. Landseers, Swiss Mountain Dogs, and Newfoundlands are typical representatives of these large breeds, as are Rottweilers and, of course, large mixed breeds that are less suited for agility or disc dog but obviously still need to get exercise. Quite a few breeds have pulling in their blood because they have been used for this purpose for centuries. In addition, Retrievers, Boxers, Doberman Pinschers, Dalmatians, and many other purebred dogs as well as large mixed breeds often find they really enjoy it.

Course or trail

An amazingly wide range of vehicles, from the rustic to the ultramodern, can be used for pulling sports. But regardless of whether you choose a normal wagon or a Sacco cart, what's critical for healthy pulling is that you use a special, well-fitting pulling harness for the dog and a suitable tug line to hitch him up. Carting, which includes drafting and driving, is done in different ways. In an obstacle course, the handler accompanies his harnessed dog over a course as he navigates around several obstacles; agility is what matters most here. A trail is a drive where the dog pulls the wagon (usually a Sacco cart) plus the driver, guided by the driver's voice commands.

Proper training

At present, a growing number of canine sports enthusiasts are introducing their dogs to carting by taking part in training programs.

Dog pulling sports demand that the dog be carefully trained in many areas, one of which is traffic safety.

Here, too, as in any other active dog sport, the dog must be fully grown before he can participate regularly. However, you certainly can and should begin training a young dog, first by getting him used to wearing the pulling harness and, later on, attaching the tug line.

And, of course, you can get an early start on practicing the appropriate signals, such as the commands for changing speed and direction.

Variations for avid runners

A surprising number of dog sports make use of pulling harnesses. In bikejoring, the dog is hitched in front of a bicycle. However, a three-wheeled trike drawn by one or two dogs is less likely to tip over. The driver stands on it and, if necessary, can pedal along. Canicross is a fairly new sport from France in which the dog, wearing a pulling harness and leash, runs ahead while his owner jogs behind. Large breeds are less suitable for this; instead, it's better for dogs who love to run.

Tip: If you would like to find out whether your dog likes pulling sports, you should only try it with professional guidance, perhaps at a dog school. Never just attach a cart or sled to the dog's collar/harness using a rope. The dog could be hurt.

At an easy trot: Dog pulling sports are becoming increasingly popular as a recreational activity for large purebred or mixed-breed dogs.

Dogs with Handicaps

Dogs with illnesses or handicaps don't have to be stay-at-homes. With individual attention, they can participate in sports and games, too.

Kimmi loves agility, even though she can't see a single obstacle or read her owner's body language. The little three-year-old Collie is blind. Kimmi was just ten weeks old when the owner first began to suspect that something was wrong with her dog. Progressive retinal atrophy was the devastating diagnosis. Degeneration of the retina would lead to total blindness—which was the case when the little dog was only four months old. It was a shock for her owner, who had dreamed of taking part in activities with her dog and now had a four-legged patient to care for. As she has discovered, though, nothing could be further from the truth, and not just when she does agility training with Kimmi. Her beautiful long-haired Collie accompanies her on long walks and romps happily with other dogs. Anyone watching the dog do this would never suspect that she's blind.

Hard to believe: Although she's blind, Kimmi even tackles the weave poles in the agility course. She does this by responding to her owner's verbal signals *"Left!"* and *"Right!"* A treat keeps her highly motivated. The dog loves agility more than anything else. Yet, the sport isn't just a way for Kimmi to have fun; it also improves her physical coordination. Life with a handicap doesn't have to be boring.

Training fosters confidence

In agility training, Kimmi has learned, step by step, to trust the voice of her owner unconditionally. The training program was basically no different than that used for other dogs, says dog trainer Anja Mack, just a little more cautious; and it was always done on-leash so that the dog could be led around. When the owner walks her dog up to an obstacle, she always gives her the signal *"Careful!"* so that Kimmi knows there is something ahead. Then her owner tells her what she has to do: *"Jump!"* for the hurdle, *"Left!"* and *"Right!"* for the weave poles. With plenty of praise and treats, she has taught Kimmi what to do at each obstacle. Now, despite her handicap, the dog takes them all: She goes through the tunnel, climbs over the A-frame, jumps over little hurdles, and even balances on the narrow dog walk—her greatest challenge. Step by step, she feels her way forward, sniffing as she goes, and navigates the course from beginning to end with her owner at her side. The bond between Edeltraud Eike and Kimmi is based on enormous mutual trust.

This way, Kimmi can even take part in the annual dog race at her dog school—always following her owner's voice!

Seniors can stay active, too

Kimmi is not the only dog to have found a suitable sport. Almost every handicap allows a dog some freedom for physical and mental activity. And, even seniors needn't spend boring days indoors, but can continue to enjoy an active lifestyle appropriate for their particular condition. In agility, for example, the requirements can be scaled back so that big jumps are no longer necessary. A growing number of dog schools even offer special courses for older dogs or those with handicaps. And, you're guaranteed to find a suitable game, whether it's the "Towel Roll" (❯ page 22), or a little "Treasure Hunt" indoors or outdoors (❯ pages 31/34).

Kimmi starts by sniffing at an obstacle, like the A-frame here. The trainer is especially pleased that the dog uses her sense of smell routinely now, because in the beginning she was so insecure that she didn't sniff at all. This has greatly improved the handicapped dog's quality of life. Now, she can find her way and move around freely, even when she is out for a walk with her owner.

"*Careful!*" says Edeltraud Eike to her female Collie before each obstacle. Then, Kimmi knows: Here's an obstacle. Next, her owner gives her the appropriate command, which the dog carries out trustingly. "*Jump!*", and over the hurdle she goes.

159

HAPPY
AND
HEALTHY

Sports and games will keep your four-legged friend fit.
They are important for an even disposition and good
physical condition. But, the right diet as well as
regular medical checkups and proper care are
also necessary to ensure that your canine
companion stays happy, energetic, and
healthy for many years to come.

A Proper Diet Keeps Your Dog Happy and Healthy

If you want your four-legged friend to have an active dog's life, you may wonder if you'll need to give her a special diet. In answering this question, think about your own situation: Even if you are an especially avid amateur athlete, you probably don't rely on performance-enhancing products; instead, you simply eat a healthy diet. That's exactly what your canine athlete needs, too.

The rib test

Just as you can feel every excess pound when you jog or hike, your dog's energy and health will suffer if you are too generous with her daily feedings. Before you really get started on a sports program, you should check to see whether your dog is at her ideal weight: Put both hands on her rib cage. If you have no trouble feeling each individual rib (1, 2, 3 . . .), her weight is probably fine. To be certain, ask your veterinarian's opinion of your dog's figure

at the next appointment. In case your dog needs to shed a few pounds, you could switch temporarily to a weight reduction diet, which contains more fiber, and start a gentle exercise program.

Easy meals in a hurry

If you want to feed your dog a balanced diet without going to a lot of fuss, then veterinarians usually recommend premium commercial dog foods. These contain all the nutrients necessary for good health. When choosing a commercial diet, it's important to pay attention to the package label. For your dog's main meals—two a day are recommended for adults—use a dog food that says "complete and balanced." Supplemental pet foods contain additional ingredients, like rice or cereals, that are only necessary when feeding an all-meat diet (even from cans). Snacks, which include the enormous assortment of treats, chew bones and the like, are suitable as food rewards in games and sports but never for regular feeding. However, they are a source of calories.

The decision whether to feed dry food (kibble) or moist (canned) food depends mainly on practical considerations: Dry food is easier to handle when you're on the go, and once opened it stays fresh longer. You should keep in mind that dry food contains much less water (less than 10 percent) than moist food (about 75 percent water). That's why dry food provides considerably more energy and, consequently, the dog needs less of it.

Because many dogs prefer moist food, simply alternate feeding both. This way, you'll be sure to please your dog's palate.

Calculate the calories: When figuring out how much to give your dog at the main meal of the day, always take into account snacks like chew bones or treats.

Proper feeding: Puppies and young dogs should be fed three or four times a day, adults twice. Important for canine athletes: Don't feed your dog in the two-hour period before engaging in an activity or immediately afterward.

Homemade with expert advice

If you don't trust commercially prepared dog food and would rather give your dog homemade or raw food, you really need professional advice to be certain you're providing the dog with adequate amounts of all the essential nutrients. You can seek advice from veterinarians or veterinary schools that offer nutritional counseling for a small fee. In addition, some laboratories will test commercial food for nutritional value and quality.

Healthy dogs are beautiful

You can even tell by looking whether or not you are feeding your dog a good diet. External signs of good health include a shiny coat, smooth (not brittle) nails, and unblemished skin. What you throw away every day in the poop bag also reveals a lot: Your dog's stools should be dry, not slimy, and have a homogenous consistency (and, thus, very little undigested material or fiber).

Special diets for health problems

Special performance diets, for instance those with high protein content, are only required by extreme canine athletes like sled dogs during the racing season (and here, every owner usually has his or her own secret recipe anyway). Otherwise, it is only necessary to switch to a special diet when the dog has health problems. Never change your dog's diet arbitrarily; instead, ask your dog's regular veterinarian for advice.

Fit and **Healthy** for Games and Sports

Exercise keeps us young and healthy; that's true for our four-legged friends, too. But sports also involve risks: overexertion, injuries, or training that is too one-sided. That's why you should approach your dog's games-and-sports program slowly, keep it varied, and pay close attention to how your dog reacts to exertion. Although we can simply stop when we are frustrated or in pain, dogs find it much more difficult to be reasonable. As a member of the pack, your dog will try to keep up at any cost, stay close when you're bicycling or jogging, and ignore growing exhaustion until she really can't go on. Besides, it's not easy for us to correctly interpret signs of exhaustion in our dogs. That's why the most important rule is to train more often for shorter periods rather than too long at one time.

Striking the right balance here depends on the dog's condition as well as the particular sport. Fifteen minutes of flyball or disc dog are far more demanding physically than half an hour of obedience, and an hour-long individual lesson requires much more from the dog than a group session where every dog may put in just 15 minutes of physical effort. Responsible canine sports trainers keep that in mind and will tell their two-legged students to take a break. You should definitely take that to heart.

Bones never forget

One of the most common mistakes of dog owners, usually made because they don't know any better, is to start exercising too soon with a young dog. A dog that is just six to eight months old may be high-spirited, but she is still not fully grown, and having her run along beside a bicycle for half an hour is too much.

Premature exercise can cause acute injuries like torn ligaments, pulled muscles, or fractures. Often, however, the dog doesn't pay the penalty until years later. Putting too much strain on the sensitive growth zones of the bones can have far-reaching consequences: A premature closure of the growth plate may cause later misalignments of the limbs and subsequent joint problems like arthritis. It can also lead to activation or worsening of degenerative diseases like hip dysplasia (HD), elbow dysplasia (ED), or osteochondrosis dissecans (OCD), which are often hereditary in dogs.

Little dogs grow up faster

That's why it is so important to introduce your four-legged friend to exercise gradually and to find out when her bones will finish growing. This is

Footloose and fancy free: Games and sports require a sensible diet and proper attention to your dog's health.

Test: **How Fit is Your Dog?**

The following questions should help you evaluate your four-legged friend's condition correctly.

My dog is . . .	small	medium	large
A ○ . . . younger than	7	6	5 years
B ○ . . . older than	7	6	5 years
C ○ . . . older than	10	8	6 years

When I put my hands on my dog's sides, I can feel her ribs . . .

A ○ . . . very well
B ○ . . . slightly
C ○ . . . not at all

Our daily walks last at least . . .

A ○ . . . 2 to 3 hours
B ○ . . . 1.5 to 2 hours
C ○ . . . 0.5 to 1 hour

My dog and I take part in athletic activities together (for example, bicycling, jogging, canine sports like agility)

A ○ Yes, even avidly (2 to 3 times per week)
B ○ Yes, about once a week or sporadically
C ○ No, we only take walks

A recent checkup at the veterinarian revealed:

A ○ Everything in order with the musculoskeletal and cardiovascular systems
B ○ Minor disorders of the musculoskeletal and/or cardiovascular system
C ○ Problems with the cardiovascular and/or the musculoskeletal system, or the dog is still too young (less than 12 to 18 months) or too old for more intense sports

INTERPRETATION

Which responses did you choose most often: A, B, or C?

(A) Tip-top shape: Your dog is a bundle of energy. However, make sure that you don't wear her out physically. Challenge your dog mentally, too, for example with searching games or puzzles.

(B) Moderately fit: What your dog needs most are sports that don't put too much stress on her bones and joints. Trotting along with you when you jog, do Nordic walking, bicycle, swim, or take short hikes is ideal exercise, if your dog enjoys it (but check with the veterinarian, first).

(C) Exercise for seniors: If your dog is reaching retirement age, you should watch her weight and participate in non-strenuous activities with her, like obedience or tracking. However, neither age nor illness is a reason to stop challenging your dog (talk with the veterinarian). Many games provide exciting mental exercise while requiring only moderate physical exertion, for example, thinking games (❯ beginning on page 90) and searching games (❯ beginning on page 30).

roughly at ten months for small dogs, one year for medium-sized dogs, and one and a half to two years for the large breeds. However, there are differences in individual development. It's best to ask your veterinarian how your dog is doing and which games and sports would be appropriate for her at this point.

Health check (not just) for active dogs

In any event, if you plan to begin an exercise program with your dog, your first stop should be the veterinary clinic. The doctor will check the dog's general health, heart, and lungs, as well as her body composition (development of the muscles, body fat, and joints). Routine blood work should also be done at regular intervals (less frequently in young animals, at least twice a year in older dogs, then, annually). If your dog starts to have difficulty moving, an X-ray examination or gait analysis can help diagnose the problem. For dogs who take part in competitive sports, there should be less time between checkups, and an annual blood test would be a good idea at any age. Incidentally, the widespread assumption that mixed-breed dogs are more robust than purebreds is untrue; that's why regular health checks are necessary for all dogs.

Shape up gradually

Tackling the agility course with an overweight dog is simply unfair, as well as being unhealthy. If your dog is chubby, you should introduce her gradually to a more athletic lifestyle. Often, just a smaller food bowl works wonders because reduced portions don't look so skimpy in it. If you can't stay the course, you should switch to a weight reduction diet for a while. Slowly increase your dog's activity level, for example, with several short walks a day that get a bit longer from week to week.

When you do this, include little exercises like "Go Around the Obstacle" (❯ page 53), have her jump up and balance on a fallen log, or try "Mountain Climbing Made Easy" (❯ pages 60/61).

PRACTICAL TIP

First Aid for Sports Injuries

Muscle pulls are not uncommon. Veterinarians recommend that you apply cold as soon as possible using a cold pack, cold spray, or a few ice cubes. Caution: Never place anything cold directly on the dog's coat. Wrap the cold pack or ice cubes in a towel. Keep the dog quiet, too. Arnica from the homeopathic medicine chest (once an hour) or Bach Rescue Remedy can provide some relief. Wait until the following day to treat with heat or anti-inflammatory gels or ointments. You still have to go to the veterinarian, though!

An obedience class is also an excellent way to get the dog moving mentally and physically again. When the dog has almost attained her ideal shape and the veterinarian gives you the green light, you can begin with more intense training, for example, with some easy bicycling (start by having her trot along as you ride five minutes and push five minutes for a few days, then ride ten minutes and push ten minutes, and so on); or your could try an agility class for beginners.

First aid and your dog's medicine chest

If you frequently engage in athletic activities with your dog, whether it's going on a hike or taking part in competitive events, you should be prepared for emergencies.

"I feel great": This dog is obviously the picture of contentment. Lying on her back with her legs up in the air—what a wonderful way to relax after a workout.

In your cellphone, store the telephone numbers of your veterinarian, a nearby veterinary clinic, and a pet ambulance. You'll be well equipped to give first aid if you keep the following supplies handy (available in the pharmacy and/or pet store).

Tweezers: With narrow, rounded tips to remove dirt, small foreign bodies, or thorns from wounds and skin, for instance paw pads.

Tick forceps: They'll help you tackle these annoying little parasites.

Scissors: Slightly curved scissors with rounded tips to cut gauze and adhesive tape or, if necessary, the hair around the edge of a wound.

Flashlight: A little penlight is very useful for examining ears, mouth, and wounds (hardware store).

Cold/Hot pack: This is helpful with injuries like pulled muscles (❯ Practical tip, page 166).

Thermometer: A digital thermometer is best. Normal temperature is 100 to 102°F (38–39°C) for adults and up to 103°F (39.5°C) for puppies.

Gauze bandages: Two or three gauze bandages about 1.5 to 3 inches (4–8 cm) wide.

Gauze pads: Several types, preferably sterile, and absorbent cotton.

Adhesive tape: 1 to 2 inches (2.5–6 cm) wide that can be cut to size.

Disinfectants: Three percent hydrogen peroxide to disinfect superficial skin wounds or abrasions contaminated with dirt or rust. Tincture of iodine to clean and disinfect wounds. Antibiotic powder or ointment for topical wound care.

Medications: Arnica pellets, Bach Rescue Remedy.

Wellness for Body and Soul

Even dogs enjoy gentle stroking that helps them let go utterly and completely, for example, after a strenuous day of training or competition, or just as an occasional moment of cuddling.

Time for tenderness

Gentle massage relaxes your dog's muscles and strengthens the bond between the two of you. A quiet atmosphere is important for this, as is the willingness of your dog to entrust herself absolutely to your hands.

Not all dogs like this sort of intense contact for more than a few minutes, right from the start. That's why you should try it out cautiously. If your dog seems to enjoy it, you can continue massaging

Paw check: If you walk a lot with your dog, you should check her paw pads regularly. Paw reflexology relaxes the entire dog—but it should first be demonstrated by a professional.

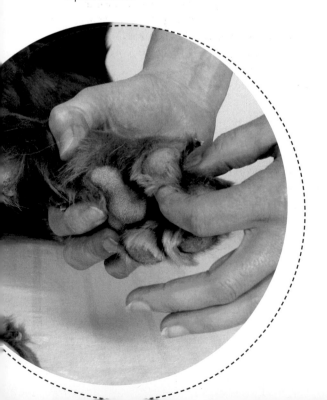

gently. If she shows signs of stress (body tense, wants to stand up, ears laid back), stop after a little bit of petting and keep trying it for a few seconds at a time at quiet moments. Today, there are physical therapists for animals who, in addition to providing a wide range of treatments, offer classes in wellness for interested dog owners. A few lessons will teach you how to give your dog a massage that is soothing and healthful.

Here are a few basics for anyone who would like to become a wellness expert. Never force your dog

›› PRACTICAL TIP

Warm up and cool down

Compulsory program before engaging in any sport: Gently warm up the dog's muscles to improve circulation. Begin about 20 to 30 minutes before you exercise or take part in an event:
- Five to ten minutes walking at an easy pace on-leash, then another five to ten minutes alternately walking and trotting. Have your dog heel when you do this.
- Run in a big circle or a figure eight for two or three minutes, gradually making the figure tighter. Follow this by having the dog weave through your legs once or twice.

Take a little longer warming up in winter. In very cold weather, put a coat on your dog so that her muscles don't cool down again too much before you begin. After any physical activity, relax by taking a quiet walk without any strenuous activity and end with a gentle massage.

Pleash don't disturb: Active dogs need time to relax, too, so give her plenty of opportunity for it. A gentle massage can help her let go if she enjoys the intense contact.

to do anything. Choose the right moment; if your dog is already relaxed in the *down* position or on her side, try a little massage. Don't give your dog a massage when she is sick. As you may know from personal experience, if you aren't feeling well or something hurts, sometimes you don't want to be touched. A sick dog who can't even tell you where it hurts is not a candidate for a massage.

Massage techniques

Good areas for massage are the muscles of the back on either side of the spine (never directly on the backbone!), the thighs, and the front legs; gently stroking the torso and legs is also good. Dogs enjoy ear and paw reflexology, too, but you should definitely have a professional demonstrate how to do

these. For a massage, the dog should be relaxed and lying on her side. To give a back massage, use only the flat part of your fingertips; applying gentle pressure, massage in small circular motions from neck to tail and back again. When you do this, the skin over the muscles should move slightly. To massage the thigh muscles, use a bit more of your fingertips. Hips, knee joints, and backbone are off limits.

When massaging the muscles of the front legs, grasp the leg above the elbow joint with one hand, placing the thumb on the muscle above. Then, move the thumb gently in small circles, ending almost at the elbow joint.

Finish by stroking with the palms of both hands, applying light pressure as you move from the dog's neck across her torso to her legs.

GAMES AND
SPORTS
AT A GLANCE

The following tables give you an overview of all the games and sports in this manual. This way, you can quickly and easily select just the right thing for you and your dog. The ages given in the table serve as a rough guide. Keep in mind your own dog's stage of development.

Game	You need	Age of the dog	What is trained	Times
Cardboard Box and Pillow Pile > pages 19/21	Treats, cardboard box, newspaper, several (sofa) pillows.	Ideal even for the youngest: Box Search from 10 to 12 weeks; Pillow Pile from 12 to 14 weeks.	Agility and persistence. Dogs who know *sit* or *down* should wait in this position for the signal to start.	One or two rounds per day. Don't let the youngest search for more than five to ten seconds; give experienced dogs a maximum of one minute.
Towel Roll > Pages 22/23	Treats, an old hand towel.	From four months for a simple version. Seniors and dogs with health problems can also do this.	The dog needs patience and agility to unroll the towel and find the treats.	No more than twice in a row, two to three times a week. Adjust the length and difficulty of the game to suit the age of the dog.
Treat Bottle > Pages 24/25	Sturdy plastic bottle, fabric cube, treat ball, treat bottle with rope (pet store), treats.	Plastic bottle from four months; treat ball from four to five months; treat bottle with rope from nine months.	Agility and persistence are needed here for the dog to get the food reward.	Don't play it every day; this way, the game stays exciting. Young dogs should only do this for a few minutes.
Treat Flip > Pages 26/27	Pieces of dry food or cheese cubes that are not too light.	Dog should be six to nine months old before you start doing this exercise with her.	The dog needs a lot of agility here. It takes discipline to keep from nibbling too soon.	Two or three minutes per session are enough. Once the dog has learned the game, don't play it more than two or three times in a row.
Treasure Hunt Indoors > Pages 31/32	An article to hide (toy, scarf), possibly leash and harness, treats.	From four months; increase the degree of difficulty according to the age. Ideal for seniors, too.	The dog learns to concentrate on searching and, then giving the article back to you.	Young dogs need to succeed in five to ten seconds. For experienced dogs, increase level of difficulty. Play once or twice a week.

Game	You need	Age of the dog	What is trained	Times
Treasure Hunt Outdoors ❯ Pages 34/35 ⬤ 🐾 🌳	A few articles (cap, scarf, glove), possibly a clicker (❯ page 40), treats.	You can start to teach this little searching game when your dog is six to nine months old.	The game requires the dog to be attentive and concentrate on you.	Include this occasionally on your walks. Let the dog take his time finding the treasure.
Retrieving ❯ Pages 36/37 ⬤ 🐾 🏠 🌳	A toy or a ball to throw, treats.	Your dog should be about six months old before you practice retrieving with her.	This trains discipline and concentration (waiting patiently, watching, surrendering the article).	One or two rounds are enough, preferably not every day. Gradually increase the level of difficulty.
Find the Treat Bag ❯ Pages 38/39 ⬤ ⬤ 🐾 🌳	Leash (or long line), harness, treat bag (or a small pouch), treats.	From about six months. You can easily create your own variations of this game.	The dog has to use her nose. Discipline is necessary, because she has to give the bag back to you.	In the beginning, she should be successful after just two or three minutes. Play one or two games three or four times per week.
Find the Scented Towel ❯ Pages 42/43 ⬤ 🐾 🏠	Cloth towel; scented pads (for example, paper towels); scents like honey or milk; possibly a drinking glass.	Depending on your dog's maturity, start teaching this game when she is 9 to 12 months old.	Sense of smell and the ability to combine two tasks (smelling, indicating the scented item).	Familiarize the dog with the scent (one or two minutes). Practice two or three times at first, later on, once or twice per week.
Lost and Found ❯ Pages 44/45 ⬤ 🐾 🌳	A leash in the beginning, an article that belongs to you, and treats.	You can start with a simple version of the game when the dog is six to nine months old.	Your dog learns to pay attention to you and to indicate an article on her own.	Practice this game for a few minutes at a time over several days; no more than two or three games in succession, two or three times a week.

	Game	You need	Age of the dog	What is trained	Times
	Scent Trail > Pages 48/49	Harness, leash, two articles to mark the beginning and end of the track, rewards.	For this fairly demanding game, your dog should be about one year old (possibly a bit younger).	Here, the dog learns to pick up a scent and concentrate on following it independently.	Patience is necessary in tracking, so that the dog can take his time searching. For beginners, lay only short tracks.
	Find the Missing Person > Pages 50/51	Harness, leash, another person, an article belonging to that person, clothespins, reward.	The dog should be about one year old before you introduce him to this demanding task.	The dog's sense of smell, powers of concentration, and the ability to work independently.	How long the dog's search lasts depends on the degree of difficulty. Allow about 10 to 20 minutes for it.
	Go Around the Obstacle > Pages 53/55	Leash (for beginners), obstacle to go around, treats.	The dog can learn to go around small obstacles once he is five to six months old.	Going around an obstacle and coming back to you demands concentration.	Even if it goes well, don't repeat too often (one to three times in a row). Can easily be incorporated into every walk.
	Weave Through My Legs > Pages 56/57	Suitable clothing (no skirts, dresses, or long coats), several treats.	From 12 to 14 weeks of age. Even seniors can quickly learn to weave through a person's legs.	Agility and good teamwork between you and your dog.	For a young dog, start with two steps, then three, and increase gradually. No more than twice in succession.
	Dog Racing > Pages 58/59	A teammate with a dog (the dogs should know each other and get along well), treats.	You can introduce racing when your dog is 9 to 12 months old.	The dog's patience and the ability to concentrate.	Only a few minutes so you don't strain the dog's patience too much. One or two rounds are enough.

Game	You need	Age of the dog	What is trained	Times
"Mountain Climbing" Made Easy > Pages 60/61	A small embankment, treats.	Low hills from six months; steeper slopes from one year (puts stress on the joints!).	Concentration. The dog learns to follow your directions and carry out your commands.	Once or twice in a row is enough. Two or three times a week at first; sporadically later on.
Jump Through the Hoop > Pages 62/63	A small, medium, or large-sized hula hoop, treats.	For puppies, those with joint problems, and elderly dogs, hold the hoop only 2 inches (5 cm) off the ground.	Coordination and agility are required (and also a little courage).	Have the dog jump two or three times in a row, at most. When training this, only practice for one or two minutes once or twice a week.
"Tree Touch" > Pages 64/65	An obstacle to touch (a tree outdoors, a wall indoors), treats, clicker and target stick (> pages 40/64).	You can start teaching this game to your dog when she is six to nine months old.	Concentration. The dog learns to go where you tell her and carry out a command there.	One to two minutes with the clicker and target stick. Don't practice the individual steps; instead, work on them one at a time.
High Five > Pages 69/71	A non-skid surface so that the dog can sit securely, treats.	The dog can begin practicing this cute trick as early as four to five months of age.	Primarily agility. Your dog learns to place her paw precisely on your hands.	Teaching this game step by step can take several days. Don't practice more than two or three times in a row per session.
Roll Over > Pages 72/73	A soft surface for the dog to roll on; treats.	From nine months to one year (the dog's stomach must be empty for this exercise > page 72!).	The dog needs agility to roll over.	Teach the exercise step by step. Run through the sequence only two or three times in a row. Do not practice this exercise every day.

	Game	You need	Age of the dog	What is trained	Times
	Jump Through My Arms ❯ Pages 74/75	Soft ground, because the dog is jumping; treats.	From 12 months. Not for seniors or dogs with joint problems.	Good fitness exercise. Your dog learns to make an agile leap through your arms.	The finished exercise takes a few days, depending on how often you practice. Don't have the dog jump more than two or three times in a row.
	Jump on My Back ❯ Pages 76/77	Soft ground, a second person, possibly clicker and target stick (❯ pages 40/64), treats.	From 12 months, so you don't put stress on the dog's joints too soon.	The dog learns to coordinate his movements when jumping, so that he lands safely on your back.	First, practice a sequence until it works consistently; don't do it more than two or three times in a row. Practicing a few minutes a day is enough.
	Go Backward ❯ Pages 78/79	Treats for rewards, clicker (❯ page 40), possibly a leash (in the beginning).	You can start training your dog to go backward when he is 9 to 12 months old.	Coordination and concentration. Important: The dog should back up in a straight line.	Teach this exercise slowly. Start by having the dog take one step backward once or twice, then two steps, and so on. Add one step per week.
	Twist ❯ Pages 80/81	Possibly a clicker and target stick (❯ pages 40/64), treats.	You can teach your dog this exercise once she is six to nine months old.	Attentiveness and coordination; ability to concentrate on performing a sequence of movements calmly.	Don't practice the individual sequences for longer than 20 seconds at a time. It could take several days of training for the dog to learn the twist.
	Jump Through My Legs ❯ Pages 82/83	Soft ground, treats (or a toy), possibly clicker and target stick (❯ pages 40/64).	From nine months to one year of age. Don't start to practice jumping until then.	Coordination and attentiveness when the dog jumps at your signal.	Don't practice more often than two or three times for 30 seconds to a minute. Do the finished exercise two or three times, at most.

Game	You need	Age of the dog	What is trained	Times
Put Away the Toy ❭ Pages 84/85	A toy, a basket or small box, clicker (❭ page 40), treats.	The dog is able to perform a sequence of actions once he is nine months to one year old.	Ability to work independently and combine two actions.	Practice each sequence about two to three minutes, not more than three times in a row. It can take several weeks to perfect the exercise.
Caps Off ❭ Pages 86/87	A cap with bill, clicker (❭ page 40), treats.	You can start training this trick when your dog is six to nine months old.	Coordination and independent action, because the dog has to pull the cap from your head.	Step by step for one or two minutes, twice in succession. If you practice twice a day, your dog can learn this trick in one to two weeks.
The Perfect Bow ❭ Pages 88/89	Possibly a clicker or target stick (❭ pages 40/64), treats.	By the time your dog is about four months old, he will be able to concentrate enough to do this exercise.	Coordination and attentiveness are needed to stay in position until you give the release word.	Train step by step, not more than two or three times in a row, for 30 seconds to a minute. One or two training sessions daily.
Shell Game ❭ Pages 91/93	At least two cups, treats.	Your dog should be 9 to 12 months old to play this tricky thinking game.	It takes a lot of concentration for the dog to pay close attention to your actions.	Start by practicing with just one cup, then try it with two (or more) cups. Once or twice per round.
Follow My Gaze ❭ Pages 94/95	Treats.	For this task, your dog should be at least four to five months old.	This game increases your dog's ability to concentrate.	Start with one to two minutes. Practice no more than two or three times in a row, once or twice a day, but don't do it every day.

Game/Sport	You need	Age of the dog	What is trained	Game/Times
Find the Right One › Pages 96/97	A few of your dog's toys that she knows by name; possibly a clicker (› page 40).	Your dog can begin to practice as early as six to nine months.	Encourages powers of deduction and the ability to concentrate on what you say.	Practice a little bit every day. Play the finished game no more than three times in a row.
A Game for Puzzle-Lovers › Pages 98/99	A wooden puzzle toy for dogs available online, clicker (› page 40), treats.	Starting at about six months.	Careful observation, powers of deduction, ability to concentrate, and agility.	Two or three times in a row. To keep the toy interesting, don't play too often.
Go to . . . › Pages 100/101	Several people your dog knows by name; treats.	Your dog should be 9 to 12 months old to do recognition work.	Ability to concentrate and memory.	In the beginning, practice 30 seconds to one minute once or twice a day. Not more than one or two rounds in a row.
Pull It Out › Pages 102/103	A treat bag (pouch) with treats; heavy twine; a low table, dresser, or similar piece of furniture.	You can train this little reasoning game once your dog is six to nine months old.	Concentration, agility, and reasoning are required here.	Slowly increase the level of difficulty. Not more than two or three times in a row. Not daily.
Jogging and Nordic Walking › Pages 109/111	Leash, harness, possibly jogging belt; for long distances, fresh water.	Small dogs from ten months; medium-sized dogs from one year; large dogs from one and a half years.	Ideal exercise and conditioning program.	In the beginning, trot for three to five minutes, then walk at an easy pace, then run again for three to five minutes, and so on.

Sport	You need	Age of the dog	What is trained	Times
Bicycling ❯ Pages 112/115	Harness, leash, possibly a bicycle dog leash, water, snack; possibly a bicycle basket/trailer for dogs.	Small dogs from ten months; medium-sized from one year; large from one and a half years.	Ideal muscle training and conditioning program for dogs who love to run.	Start by having the dog trot along for three to five minutes; then, walk at an easy pace; then, trot again, and so on.
Hiking with Your Dog ❯ Pages 116/117	Harness, leash, fresh water, a little food for the dog, paw protection, possibly a backpack.	From ten months for a small dog to about one and a half years for large dogs (ask the vet!).	Stamina and fitness, if you follow a sensible training program. Strengthens the bond between you and your dog.	Start training with 15 to 30 minutes of hiking for a full-grown dog; slowly increase the trip length.
Water Sports ❯ Pages 118/121	Water toy, towel, life vest for the dog; at the ocean, fresh water for drinking.	You can even get puppies used to the water by playing games.	A relaxed, safe program of aquatic training will improve your dog's condition and stamina.	Slowly increase swimming practice; well-trained dogs can swim along longer with you. Always keep an eye on your dog!
Horseback Riding with Your Dog ❯ Pages 122/123	Long line, bicycle (as a substitute horse, in the beginning), leash, treats.	For rides lasting more than 15 minutes at a walking pace, the dog should be fully grown.	Stamina and condition as well as willingness to cooperate with you.	In the beginning, the dog can walk along beside you for about 15 minutes (on the leash, led by another person); later on, rides can last several hours.
Agility ❯ Pages 130/133	Toys and treats for the training.	Agility training can be started when the dog is about eight to nine months old.	Condition, agility, concentration, discipline, and a strong bond with the owner.	Introduce it playfully with group lessons, for example, one hour per week. Competitive athletes train more often.

Sport	You need	Age of the dog	What is trained	Times
Disc Dog ❯ Pages 134/135	Special flying discs. Elite athletes wear protective vests.	Professional training with fully grown dog. Get young dogs used to playing with a flying disc.	Stamina, agility, concentration, and harmonious teamwork with the human partner.	Play for one or two minutes occasionally; at advanced levels, have short training sessions (five to ten minutes) several times a week.
Flyball ❯ Pages 136/137	Lots of balls made especially for flyball; they should be the right size for the dog.	Light training with a young dog. Professional training with a fully grown dog.	Agility, condition, and stamina; enjoyment of retrieving and discipline.	Young dogs: one or two minutes of ball training (no jumps, only retrieving). For professional training in a group, 10 to 15 minutes per dog.
Canine Freestyle ❯ Pages 140/141	Music, clicker, target stick (❯ pages 60/64), props like hat or scarf; for performances, possibly costumes.	Begin training playfully at four months. Also for older dogs and those with health problems.	The dog learns to pay close attention to her human and to cooperate. Gentle exercise.	Because this sport consists of many little tricks, you can always fit in two or three minutes of training occasionally.
Search ❯ Pages 142/143	Tracking harness, special leash, scent article, somebody who will hide clothespins (marking), rewards.	Start practicing by making a game of it, for example, by just playing hide-and-seek.	Sense of smell, concentration, close cooperation with the handler, discipline.	Nose work is very demanding for dogs, so just a few minutes of training are enough in the beginning.
Obedience ❯ Pages 144/147	Leash, clicker, possibly target stick, treats, toys; for pros, traffic cones, wooden dumbbells, hurdles.	Young dogs can begin with simple training, for example, in a club.	Concentration, cooperation, discipline, and harmonious body control.	Ten to 15 minutes once or twice a week. Individual exercises when you have a moment.

Sport	You need	Age of the dog	What is trained	Times
Tracking ❯ Pages 148/149	Tracking harness, leash, scent articles for the track, clothespins or flags as markers, treats.	There are classes even for young dogs.	Sense of smell, concentration, and discipline.	Weekly training classes usually last one hour (dog schools, clubs), and every dog sniffs for one to three tracks.
Canine Search and Rescue ❯ Pages 150/151	A lot of time for training and a healthy dog that is not too small.	Training only in clubs. Young dogs can start at about four to five months; preferably not older than three years.	Sense of smell, coordination, concentration, and the bond with the handler.	Training usually requires several hours a week; frequent weekend workshops are usual.
Sled Dog Racing and Nordic Style ❯ Pages 152/153	Depending on the sport, a sled or pulk and the appropriate accessories. Can be done with one or two dogs.	Training begins when the dog is young. Fitness training in a team usually starts at 12 months.	Physical condition and close cooperation between handler and dog.	Training can be very time-consuming. This is not just a recreational activity, but rather a way of life.
Turnier-hundesport ❯ Pages 154/155	Athletic attire, leash, motivational toys, treats.	Dogs must be at least 15 months old before they can begin to compete.	Obedience, agility, condition, cooperation, and a bond with the handler.	Training in a group at least once a week; can also be more often, depending on athletic ambitions.
Dog Pulling Sports ❯ Pages 156/157	A special pulling harness, tug line, a cart	Wait until the dog is fully grown to practice pulling a cart (longer distances).	Condition, stamina, coordination, and cooperation.	Dog pulling sports are frequently taught in workshops; some clubs also offer regular training.

Tips for **Dog Photography**

Dog owners love photos that show their dogs in action. Unfortunately, these shots are the most difficult to capture, but with a few tricks everyone can take better pictures.

Try to guess how many photos I took for this book. One thousand, two thousand, five thousand? Wrong: I clicked the shutter release about ten thousand times! That's because this book is all action. The only time you'll find dogs sitting or lying down is when that was a part of the exercise. Then, one or two shots were all it took, and the photo was in the can. After that, the fun began— and every dog owner knows what this kind of photography is like: The dog is cut off, out of focus, photographed from the rear, too dark, too light—or else, all the settings are right, but the dog is doing something completely different or nothing at all. Then, you resort to something that no dog photographer can be without: Treats. The more

demanding the task, the more delectable the treats. The rewards ranged from homemade ground liver pancakes to cooked bits of chicken, or even entire gourmet dishes. But without the active support of the dog owner, it would still have taken twice as long. That's why I first had a long talk with the dog owners—even when pressed for time—so I could win them over.

The Sorrows and Joys of an Animal Photographer

Eventually, though, I wanted to take the pictures before the weather turned bad, the sun got too high in the sky, or the heat became unbearable.

In summer, I start photographing as early in the day as possible because the light is best in the morning (or late afternoon): The sun isn't strong yet, so the light is softer. Besides, when the temperature is lower, I'm not always looking at dogs with their tongues hanging out.

The final important point before actually taking photographs is the right surroundings. Wire fences, power lines, and houses in the background can ruin a beautiful photo, so it's better to walk a little further before starting to shoot. And, of course, kneeling or lying on the ground! An animal photographer should, in the truest sense of the word, see eye to eye with his subject because when you photograph your dog from above, the proportions are all wrong. When I was taking photos of small dogs in action, I spent most of my time crawling around on the ground.

Now, with automatic settings, you can just shoot away and you'll be sure to get a few successful pictures.

For action photography, however, an understanding of shutter speed and aperture, plus a camera with a fast shutter release, is indispensable.

1. A tough job: Even canine models don't have it easy. Sioux has to sprint umpteen times before the photo is finally in the can. But, at least he gets paid right away—in the form of tasty treats.

2. Ready! Shoot!: After taking a break to play with his master, Sioux is motivated again. He dives over the hurdle and I press the shutter release. Did I get the cover photo this time?

To take the cover photo, for instance, I needed to use a shutter speed of 1/2,000 second in order to get the flying dog in focus. Sioux, the dog in the photo, made about 50 sprints, but 10 times he shot past the hurdle; 15 times he didn't jump over at the exact spot I had in mind; 12 pictures were fuzzy; and in 8 photos, he had a funny look or had the disc upside down in his mouth. That left just five photos, only two of which I liked. That's why, in this age of digital photography, it's better to take a few extra photos, sort through them carefully, and, then, enjoy your (hopefully) successful results.

3. Over the hurdle: Sioux jumped over the hurdle and I photographed the various stages of his leap. Now, we are both exhausted. Sioux is happy, and my back hurts . . .

Index

Page numbers in **bold** indicate photos

Addresses

American Kennel Club (AKC)
8051 Arco Corporate Drive, Suite 100
Raleigh, NC 27617-3390
919-233-9767
www.akc.org

Canadian Kennel Club (CKC)
200 Ronson Drive, Suite 400
Etobicoke, Ontario M9W 5Z9, Canada
416-675-5511
www.ckc.ca

German Kennel Club *(Verband für das Deutsche Hundewesen, VDH)*
Westfalendamm 174
44141 Dortmund, Germany
www.vdh.de

Humane Society of the United States
2100 L Street NW
Washington, DC 20037
202-452-1100
www.humanesociety.org

United Kennel Club (UKC)
100 E. Kilgore Road
Kalamazoo, MI 49002-5584
269-343-9020
www.ukcdogs.com

World Canine Organization
(Fédération Cynologique Internationale, FCI)
Place Albert 1er, 13
B-6530 Thuin, Belgium
www.fci.be

Addresses on the Internet

Agility:
North American Dog Agility Council (NADAC)
www.nadac.com

United States Dog Agility Association (USDAA)
www.usdaa.com

Canine Freestyle:
World Canine Freestyle Organization (WCFO)
www.worldcaninefreestyle.org

Canine Freestyle Federation (CFF)
www.canine-freestyle.org

Canine Search and Rescue:
American Rescue Dog Association (ARDA)
www.ardainc.org

National Association for Search and Rescue
(NASAR)
www.nasar.org

Disc Dog:
Skyhoundz
www.skyhoundz.com

Flyball:
North American Flyball Association (NAFA)
www.flyball.org

Sled Dog Racing and Nordic Style:
International Federation of Sleddog Sports (IFSS)
www.sleddogsport.com

International Sled Dog Racing Association (ISDRA)
www.isdra.org

Water sports:
Canine Water Sports
www.caninewatersports.com

Dog sports, organized (Information on obedience, tracking, agility, Canine Good Citizen):
American Kennel Club (AKC)
www.akc.org

Australian Shepherd Club of America (ASCA)
www.asca.org

Canadian Kennel Club (CKC)
www.ckc.ca

Mixed Breed Dog Clubs of America
www.mbdca.org

United Kennel Club (UKC)
www.ukcdogs.com

World Canine Organization
www.fci.org

Books for Additional Information

American Kennel Club. *The American Kennel Club Dog Care and Training, 2nd ed.* New York: Howell Book House, 2002.

Baer, Ted. *Communicating With Your Dog, 2nd. ed.* Hauppauge, New York: Barron's Educational Series, 1999.

Birmelin, Immanuel. *How Dogs Think: A Guide to a Beautiful Relationship.* Metro Books, 2006.

Bonham, Margaret H. *Introduction to Dog Agility, 2nd ed.* Hauppauge, New York: Barron's Educational Series, 2009.

Ludwig, Gerd. *Fun and Games With Your Dog.* Hauppauge, New York: Barron's Educational Series, 1996.

Ludwig, Gerd. *Practical Handbook: Dogs.* Hauppauge, New York: Barron's Educational Series, 2005.

Ludwig, Gerd. *Sit! Stay! Train Your Dog the Easy Way.* Hauppauge, New York: Barron's Educational Series, 2008.

Mehus-Roe, Kristin. *Canine Sports & Games.* North Adams, Massachusetts: Storey Publishing, 2009.

Pryor, Karen. *Don't Shoot the Dog! The New Art of Teaching and Training.* New York: Bantam Books, 1999.

Pryor, Karen. *Getting Started: Clicker Training for Dogs.* Waltham, Massachusetts: Sunshine Books, 2004.

Schlegl-Kofler, Katharina. *The Complete Guide to Dog Training.* Hauppauge, New York: Barron's Educational Series, 2008.

Schmidt-Röger, Heike. *300 Questions About Dogs.* Hauppauge, New York: Barron's Educational Series, 2006.

Snovak, Angela Eaton. *Guide to Search and Rescue Dogs.* Hauppauge, New York: Barron's Educational Series, 2004.

Magazines
AKC Family Dog
American Kennel Club
1-800-490-5675
www.akc.org/pubs

AKC Gazette
American Kennel Club
1-800-533-7323
www.akc.org/pubs

Dog Fancy
BowTie Magazines
3 Burroughs Street
Irvine, CA 92618
949-855-8822
www.dogchannel.com/dog.magazines

DogWatch
P.O. Box 420235
Palm Coast, FL 32142-0235
1-800-829-5574

FCI Magazine
(in English, French, German, and Spanish)
www.fci.be/magazine.aspx

Important Information

The recommendations in this manual apply to normal dogs with no developmental or personality problems. If you adopt an adult dog, you must be aware that he already has been influenced to a considerable degree by humans. You should watch the dog carefully, including how he behaves toward people. If the dog is from an animal shelter, the staff there will probably be able to tell you something about the dog's background and his idiosyncrasies. Some dogs, because of bad experiences with people, have behavior problems and may also have a tendency to bite. These dogs should only be adopted by experienced dog owners. Even with dogs that are well trained and carefully supervised, there is always a chance that they will damage the property of others or even cause accidents. It is always advisable to make sure you have adequate insurance coverage.

Acknowledgments

A book is always a team effort, and this book seems to me to be an especially vivid case in point. Page by page, it demonstrates the willingness of so many dogs and their owners to participate enthusiastically in games and sports. From the bottom of my heart, I thank everyone who helped out with the time-consuming—but always enjoyable—photo shoots. Our cover dog Jumping Sioux (a Nova Scotia Duck Tolling Retriever) and his owner Klaus Friedrich from the "Hundefreunde Thann" dog club deserve a special mention here. Engaging in activities with dogs requires certain basic knowledge. In addition, games and dog sports have rules to ensure fair play and protect the health of participants. Many experts have contributed the necessary know-how in these areas, and, for this, I would like to thank them again most sincerely. I would especially like to mention here veterinarians Dr. Eva Demmel and Dr. Babara Schwarzmann of Animal Rescue Munich. Naturally, I also thank the entire GU team and my editor, Gabriele Linke-Grün, for their tremendous inspiration and patience—a wonderful topic like this is simply a joy for all involved. In working with photographer Thomas Brodmann and "my" dog trainer Anja Mack, I have also been privileged to experience just how much the companionship of dogs can motivate human teams. I have had an incredible amount of fun with Anja—and often with my female Irish Terrier Amy—figuring out how best to design and present the games. The many photos in this book testify to Thomas Brodmann's willingness to follow us at any time in search of playful dogs as well as his eye for the perfect moment. And, without Anja Mack's extensive knowledge, her profound and sensitive understanding of the canine soul, her infinite patience, and her network of contacts, this book would never have been possible. Thank you, Anja!

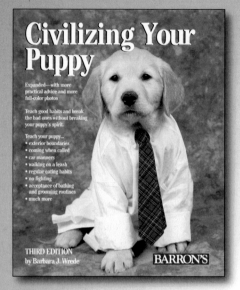

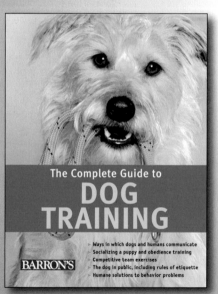
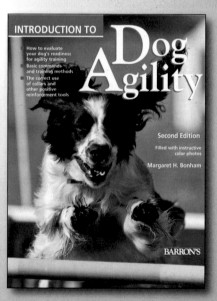

Picture Credits

All photos in this book were taken by Thomas Brodmann, with the exception of:

animals–digital/Hagedorn: 122, 123, 168, 179–4; Oliver Giel: 157; Manfred Knaller: 191–1, 191–2, 191–3; Ulrich Neddens: 154, 155–1, 155–2, 181–4; Picani/Steininger: 156, 181–5; Karin Stifter: 143–1, 143–2, 143–3.

Program Director: Christof Klocker

Managing Editor: Nadja Harzdorf

Editor: Gabriele Linke-Grün

Design: Nadja Harzdorf, Luise Heine, Gabriele Linke-Grün

Picture Editors: Adriane Andreas, Nadja Harzdorf, Gabriele Linke-Grün Alexandra Dimitrijevic (Cover)

Cover design and layout: independent Medien-Design, Munich

First edition for the United States, its territories and dependencies, and Canada published in 2010 by Barron's Educational Series, Inc.

English translation by Mary Lynch.

German edition by: Kirsten Wolf.

Published originally under the title
Hunde Spiel & Sport
© Copyright 2009 by Gräfe und Unzer Verlag GmbH, München

All inquiries should be addressed to:
Barron's Educational Series, Inc.
250 Wireless Boulevard
Hauppauge, NY 11788
www.barronseduc.com

ISBN-13: 978-0-7641-4497-4
ISBN-10: 0-7641-4497-9

Library of Congress Catalog No.: 2010003410

Library of Congress Cataloging-in Publication Data
Wolf, Kirsten.
    [Hunde. English]
    Games and sports for dogs / Kirsten Wolf. —
1st ed.
        p. cm.
        Includes index.
        ISBN-13: 978-0-7641-4497-4
        ISBN-10: 0-7641-4497-9
      1. Dogs—Training. I. Title.
        SF431.W66513 2010
        636.7′0887—dc22   2010003410

Printed in China
9 8 7 6 5 4 3 2 1